D0276523

Pelham Books
LONDON

COMPILED BY IAN MORRISON

Intersport: Rules and Equipment of the Game
compiled by Ian Morrison

First published in Great Britain by
Pelham Books
27 Wrights Lane
London W8 5TZ

Morrison, Ian
Intersport Rules and Equipment of the Game.
1. Sports
I. Title
796 GV704

ISBN 0-7207-1738-8
ISBN 0-7207-1760-4 Pbk

Designed, edited and produced by
First Editions
27 Palmeira Mansions, Church Road,
Hove, East Sussex, England BN3 2FA

Printed in England by
Redwood Burn, Trowbridge
Phototypeset by
Presentia Art, Horsham
Origination by Contemporary Litho, London

Contents

Introduction

Attempting to define "sport" has never been easy. How can you compare the leisurely actions of the snooker and bowls player with the exertions of the marathon runner or rugby forward? But each and every sport no matter whether gracefully genteel or downright dangerous is bonded together by one common characteristic . . . *competition.*

Everyone knows Bill Shankly's famous quotation about soccer: "Some people say it's a matter of life and death, in fact it's much more important than that."

And while the *Oxford Dictionary* quite properly specifies sport as – *amusement, diversion, fun,* anyone who plays a game seriously realises it is more than that rather innocent explanation.

Yes, competition is the essential element of sport, the testing of one's capabilities against another's. Being sport and not war, however, decrees that it must be done in a civilised, dignified fashion.

And for that you need rules.

Some sports who take themselves very seriously – and why shouldn't they – don't have rules. They have laws. So you have the laws of Rugby Union (and of Eton Fives) and the laws of Bowls. And, of course, the laws of Cricket.

It sounds a bit terrifying . . . transgress and you could find yourself in the dock at the Old Bailey. But the more complex the game, the more rigidly the rules, or laws, need to be applied. And to be fair, Rugby Union, Bowls and Cricket are generally very well run, sporting pastimes.

The purpose of this book is to explain those seemingly complex rules and laws in simple, straightforward terms. We have listed 20 of the world's major sports in alphabetical order, from American Football to Volleyball.

Diagrams have been used wherever possible to offer visual help on the more contentious points: such

as the no-ball in cricket and the methods of dismissal in baseball.

We have set out each sport under uncomplicated headings – For a start, its *objectives,* in other words how it's played, by how many, how you score and how long it lasts. Then we look at *playing area,* the *rules* and the sort of *clothing* and *equipment* you will need.

Here and there we have included some interesting little facts which would make good Trivial Pursuit questions – did you know precisely 16 *goose* feathers were used in the making of a shuttlecock?

Overall, our one aim has been to make sport easier to understand, both for the competitor and for the follower. It's frustrating to watch television or stand on the touchline and have a potentially fine spectacle spoilt because you don't fully comprehend what is happening and why.

We hope that once you have read *Rules and Equipment of the Game* you will know, if not all the answers, at least the ones that matter.

Intersport is a group of the world's foremost independent sports shops who offer you real choice, real advice and real style. There are over 200 shops in the UK alone, offering a fabulous range of sportswear by leading manufacturers such as Nike, Patrick, Tecno pro, Puma, Slazenger, Hi Tec, Dunlop, Umbro, Mitre, Speedo and Etirel. Whatever your sporting or leisure interests the Intersport mark means quality, value, reliability and experience.

American Football

American football is a ball game played by 2 teams with 11 players. Because it is such a tactical game, team squads can consist of up to 40 members, any of whom can replace another player during the game.

The sport was first played, in crude form, in the early 17th century when English colonists introduced their own form of football. Two hundred years later American colleges started playing rugby and it was from this sport that American Football developed. The real evolution of the game began in 1880 with many changes from the game of rugby, notably the replacement of the scrummage by the scrimmage. Over the next 20 years American Football really developed its own identity. The first professional match was held at Latrobe, Pennsylvania on 31 August 1895.

Object

To cross your opponents' line with the ball (a touchdown) and/or to score goals by kicking the ball between the posts. Points are scored for touchdowns and goals and the object is to score more points than your opponents.

Duration

A game is divided into 4 quarters, each lasting 15 minutes actual playing time. The time is recorded only when the ball is in play. Because of this, most games last in the region of 2 to 3 hours. There is an interval of 15 minutes at half time, and intervals of 1 minute between the 1st and 2nd, and 3rd and 4th quarters. If the scores are level at the end of normal time an extra 15 minutes overtime is played. The 1st score decides the winner and ends the match. If, after the extra 15 minutes the scores are still level, the game is tied. Each team is allowed 3 time-outs per half when the coach can call a halt to proceedings for a tactical team talk.

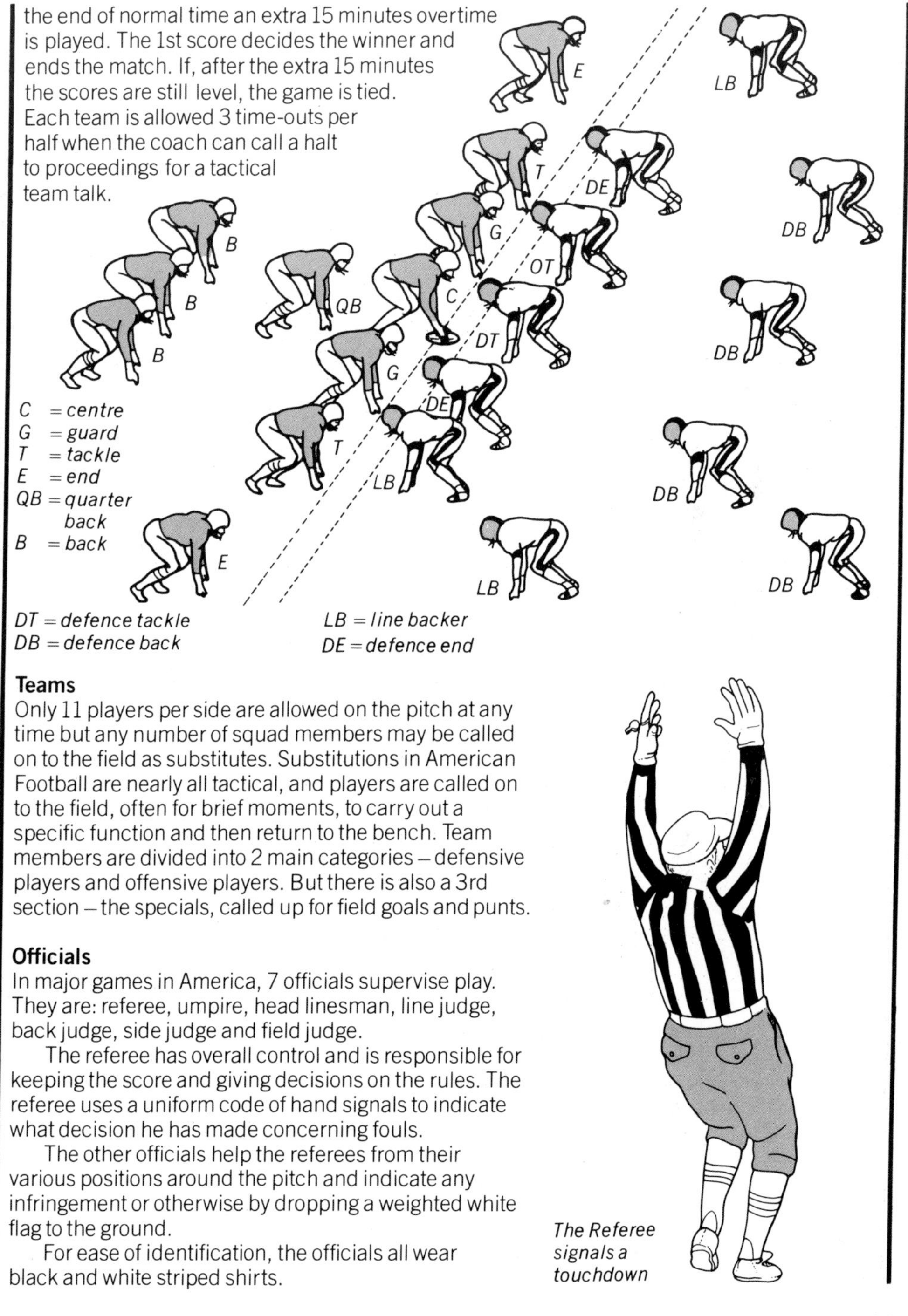

Teams

Only 11 players per side are allowed on the pitch at any time but any number of squad members may be called on to the field as substitutes. Substitutions in American Football are nearly all tactical, and players are called on to the field, often for brief moments, to carry out a specific function and then return to the bench. Team members are divided into 2 main categories – defensive players and offensive players. But there is also a 3rd section – the specials, called up for field goals and punts.

Officials

In major games in America, 7 officials supervise play. They are: referee, umpire, head linesman, line judge, back judge, side judge and field judge.

The referee has overall control and is responsible for keeping the score and giving decisions on the rules. The referee uses a uniform code of hand signals to indicate what decision he has made concerning fouls.

The other officials help the referees from their various positions around the pitch and indicate any infringement or otherwise by dropping a weighted white flag to the ground.

For ease of identification, the officials all wear black and white striped shirts.

The Referee signals a touchdown

Ball
Made of leather and similar in shape, but smaller than, a rugby ball. The diameter is approximately 7in (17.78cm) at the centre and it is about 12in (30.48cm) long. It weighs between 14-15oz (396.9-425.3g) and is inflated to 12½-13½psi.

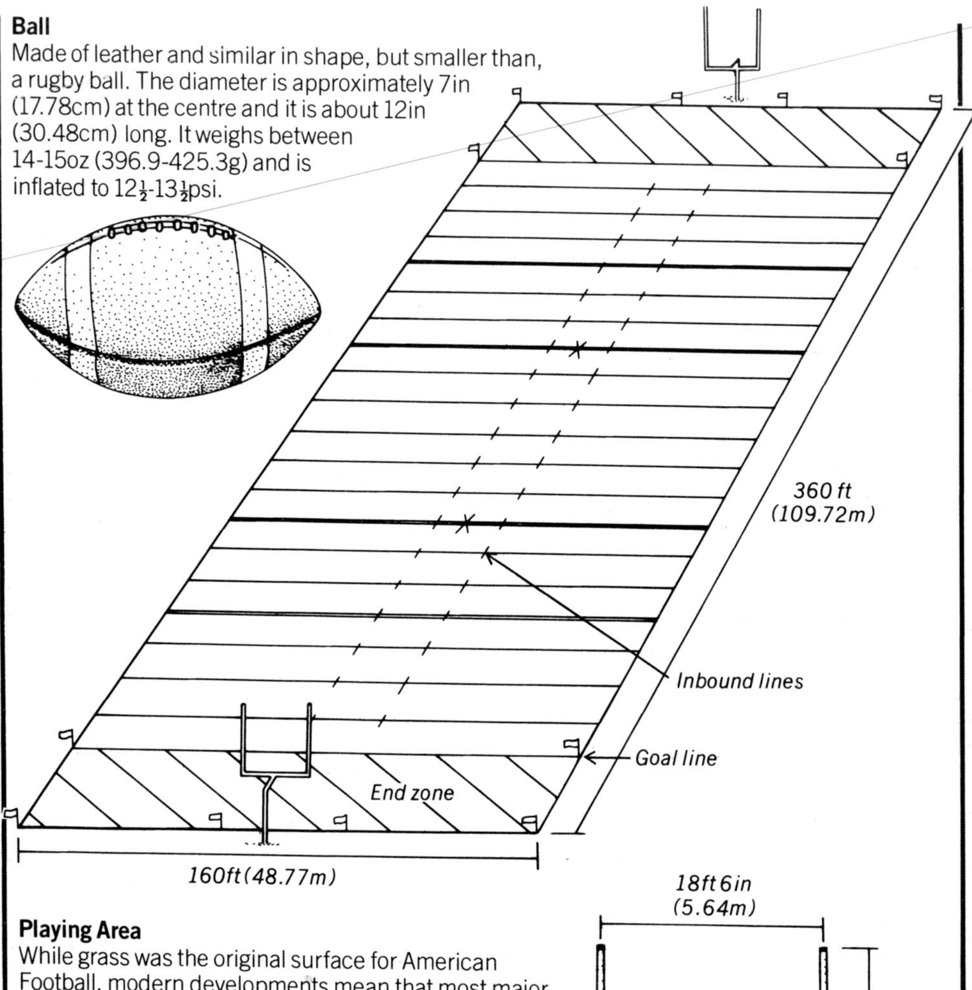

Playing Area
While grass was the original surface for American Football, modern developments mean that most major clubs in the United States play on artificial surfaces.

The field is uniform in size: 100yd (91.44m) long and 160ft (48.77m) wide. Lines, at 5yd (4.57m) intervals, are drawn across the pitch in grid fashion. The goal line indicates the end of the pitch, but, beyond each goal line, is an area the full width of the pitch and 10yd (9.14m) deep. This is the end zone, and the extreme of it is called the end line. In the middle of the end line are goalposts 18ft 6in (5.64m) apart. At one time they were 'H' shaped like rugby posts, but as the ball passes only between the area above the crossbar they have become more 'Y' shaped. The uprights and crossbar protrude from a stanchion placed 6ft (1.83m) behind the end line so the crossbar and uprights are level with the end line. The crossbar is 10ft (3.05m) above the ground.

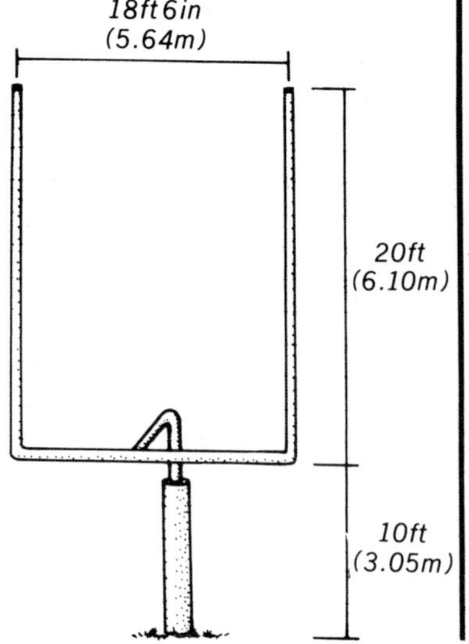

Starting Play

A toss of a coin decides which team kicks off. Play starts from the 35yd (32m) line when the ball is kicked into the opponents' half. They collect the ball and attempt to advance upfield by at least 10yd (9.14m) in four attempts. These are called downs. If they do not advance that distance they give the ball to their opponents. If they are successful in making ground in their 4 downs, they are allowed another 4, and so on. If it seems unlikely a team will make the 10 yards in their 4 downs, rather than hand over possession they will punt the ball upfield, thus hoping to force the opponents to start their attack from deep in their own half.

Kick offs

Scoring

The aim is to get the ball into your opponents' end zone for a touchdown. Unlike rugby the ball does not have to be touched down – it needs only to be carried over the line. Also, as forward passing is allowed in American Football, a player can stand in the end zone and if he catches the ball he is said to have made a touchdown.

All touchdowns are worth 6 points. Following each touchdown a conversion attempt is made from underneath the posts – and is worth an additional point. Field goals are worth 3 points and these are normally attempted when a team feels it is not going to make its 10 yards. The ball is 'snapped' back for a player to place on the ground for his specialist kicker to quickly attempt to kick over the crossbar.

Field goals can often be scored from as far away as 50yd (45.72m). The other method of scoring is if a player on the defensive is forced to carry the ball over his own goal line. He gives away a 'safety', worth 2 points to the opposing team.

A tee may be used for a place kick or another player is permitted to hold the ball.

Blocking, tackling and scrimmaging

Blocking forms an integral part of the game . . . as the offensive player wards off the attempt of a defensive player to get to the ball carrier. If the ball carrier is tackled by a defender, who must use his body and arms only, a *scrimmage* takes place. The opposing set of players (minimum of 7 per team) line up facing each other about 1ft (30.5cm) apart. The centre of the team in possession snaps the ball back to his quarter-back who has previously informed his team mates about his intended plan.

Tackling

Fouls

As American Football is a game of advancement up the field, infringements of laws result in the offending team receiving a distance penalty which moves play nearer to their goal line by 5, 10 or 15 yards. Five yard penalties are normal for offside or deliberate delay of play, whereas a 15 yard penalty would be for rough play.

A player may not knee or strike an opponent

A player may not hit or trip an opponent below the knee

Offside

A player is offside if he advances beyond the line of scrimmage before the ball is passed by the centre to quarterback. The penalty for an offside offence is 5 yards.

These rules are for the professional game in the United States. College football and the Canadian game differ slightly.

Scrimmage line

Equipment

American Football is a highly physical game, so players need a great deal of protection. The helmet with its attached facemask is the most important item of equipment.

Padding underneath the player's shirt gives protection to the shoulders, elbows, arms, ribs, and forearms. Below-the-waist protection is given by hip pads, thigh pads, knee pads and shin pads.

Athletics

Athletics is a diverse sport taking in many disciplines. Broadly speaking it is divided into 2 categories – track events, and field events. But cross-country running and road walking are also encompassed under the heading of athletics. Track athletics is divided into sprinting, middle-distance running and hurdling, and long-distance running. Field events are divided into throwing and jumping categories.

Athletics, in one form or other, dates back to the ancient Greek Olympic Games in the 13th-century BC. But organised athletics, similar to today's competition, goes back to 1849 when competitions were held at the Woolwich Military Academy in London. The first Modern Olympics, still regarded as an athlete's supreme test, were at Athens in 1896.

First regarded as an outdoor sport, athletics is now all year round with indoor arenas all over the world.

Object

The object of all athletics events is to beat your opponent(s) either by jumping or throwing further or running or walking faster.

The starter

Teams
Athletes compete individually for personal glory, but their efforts often win points for a team. The Olympics are basically an individual competition whereas the World Cup and European Cup are team events.

Officials
All running races are started by an official starter who ensures all athletes are in the correct position behind the starting line. Times are usually recorded electronically, but timekeepers still make a manual check in case of a breakdown. Judges take up positions around the track to make sure athletes remain in the correct lane and, in the case of relay races, to ensure the handover is correct. In field events, judges have to determine if jumps or throws have been correctly made, and also take the necessary measurements. An athletics meeting calls for a great many skilled judges and officials as so many events take place simultaneously.

Track
Most tracks were originally grass, but these were gradually replaced by cinder tracks and today, at top class level, the tracks are synthetic and far faster.

The track is 400m (437.44yd) in circumference and oval shaped. Eight lanes, each at least at 1.22m (4ft) wide, are marked on the track and, in sprint races, runners must keep within these lines. A common finishing line is indicated, normally in front of the main grandstand. All races are run in an anti-clockwise direction so the runner has the bend to his left. The relay takeover zones are also marked.

8 7 6 5 4 3 2 1

4ft (1.22m) 4ft (1.22m) 4ft (1.22m) 4ft (1.22m) 4ft (1.22m) 4ft (1.22m)

Within the confines of the track, or sometimes just outside it, are the field event areas. The javelin has caused problems in recent years as throwers can throw the full length of the stadium. There is a move for the event to be either moved away from the stadium or, as has been tried, the centre of gravity of the javelin has been altered to reduce the distance thrown.

Lanes
All the individual races shorter than 800m are run completely in lanes. Also run in lanes is the first bend of the 800m and the first three bends of the 4 x 400m relay. Lanes are decided by lot. Any competitor who deliberately leaves his lane shall be disqualified; if the offence was not deliberate, disqualification is at the referee's discretion.

Marks
These may be placed on or beside the track only for relay races.

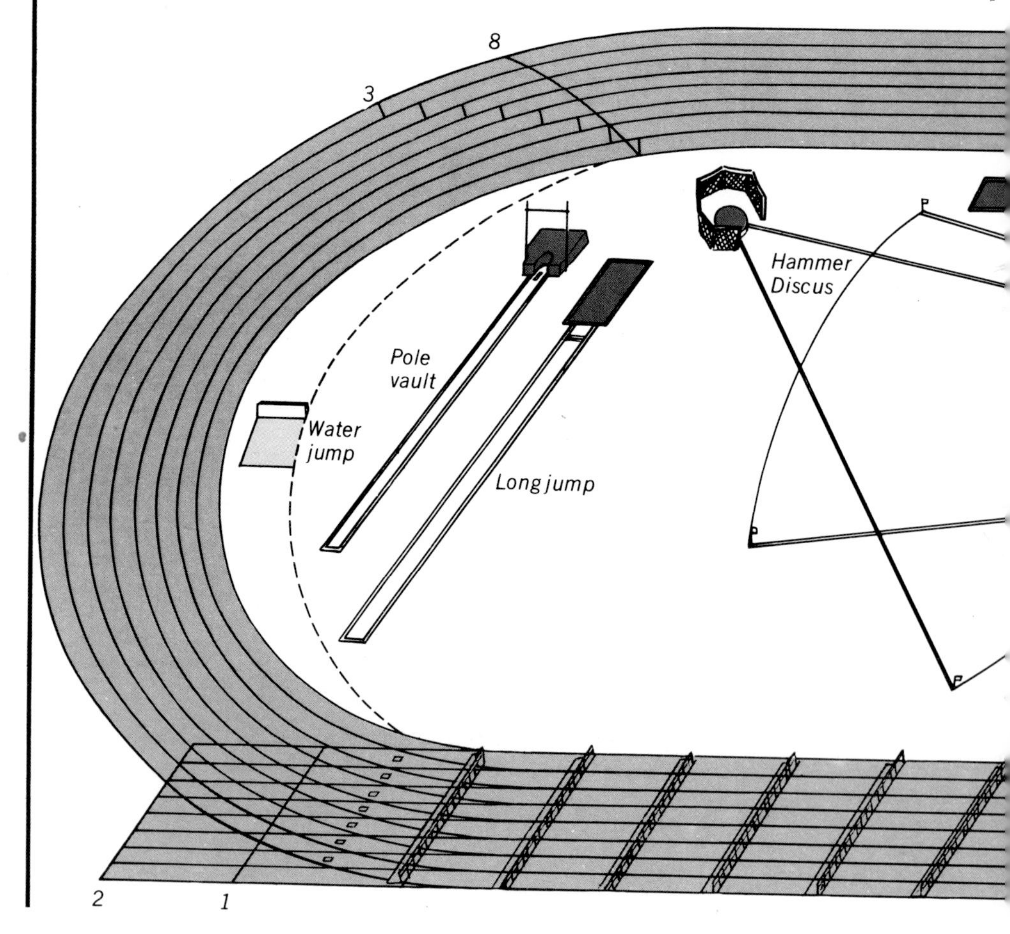

Starts

1 100m & 100m hurdles
2 110m hurdles
3 200m
4 400m & 400m hurdles
5 800m
6 1500m
7 3000m steeplechase
8 5000m
9 10,000m

Indoor tracks

Because of the limitations of space indoor tracks are slightly different, although the rules of the events remain the same. The short sprints consist only of 50/60m and such events like the hammer, discus and javelin are not staged indoors. Indoor tracks are wooden or artificial surface and are often banked at each bend. They are usually 200m in length, but do vary especially in the USA.

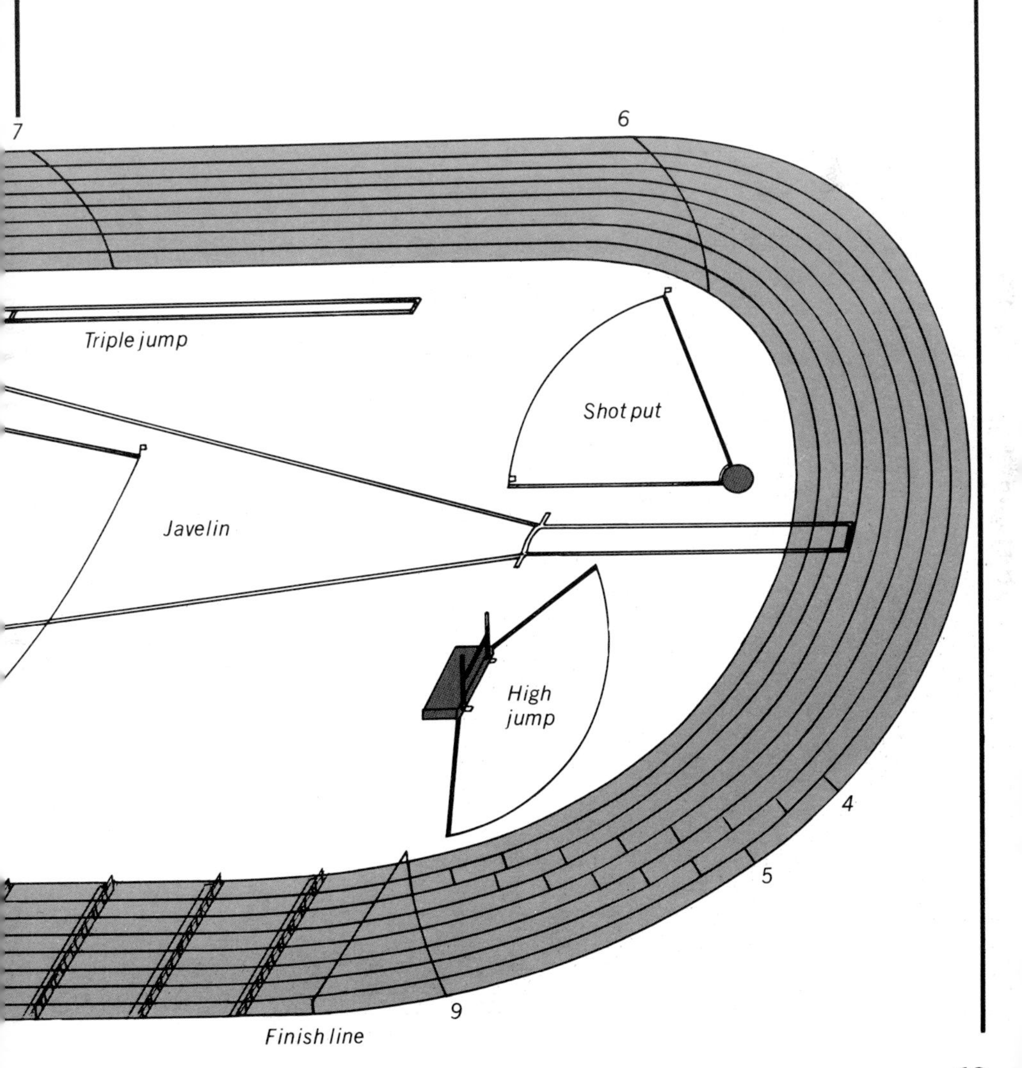

The Events

Sprints

The 100m, 200m, and 400m races are regarded as sprints. Both men and women contest all 3 events and competitors must remain in their lanes throughout the race. The competitors must start in starting blocks fixed into the track. These are wired to the electronic timing device, and also trigger off a false start light if a runner sets off before the sound of the gun. Any runner having 2 false starts is disqualified. This applies to all running events. The runners are staggered in 200m and 400m races to take into account the varying distance each must run round the bends.

Middle Distance

Middle distance races comprise the 800m, 1500m, and 3000m. The 800m has a staggered start and all runners have to remain in their lanes until they have rounded the first bend, then all runners can break for the best position. The 1500m starts near the beginning of the back straight, the mile starts just before the main starting line, and the 3000m starts at the end of the back straight. The curve start line used for all these is designed to prevent the runners bumping.

Long Distance

The 5000m and 10,000m races are the 2 long distance track races. The former starts at the end of the back straight and the runners complete 12½ laps of the track. In the 10,000m runners start at the main starting line and complete 25 laps.

In all races of more than one lap, a bell is rung as each runner crosses the line at the start of his final lap.

Marathon Running

The marathon is a road race, covering a standard distance of 26 miles 385 yards (42.195km). In international competitions, athletes start inside the main stadium and then make their way immediately on to the open road, returning to the stadium to complete a final lap or more inside. Organised marathons, like the London Marathon, are entirely on the open road and start at one point, and finish at another. Because surfaces and circuits are different for each marathon course, official world records are not kept.

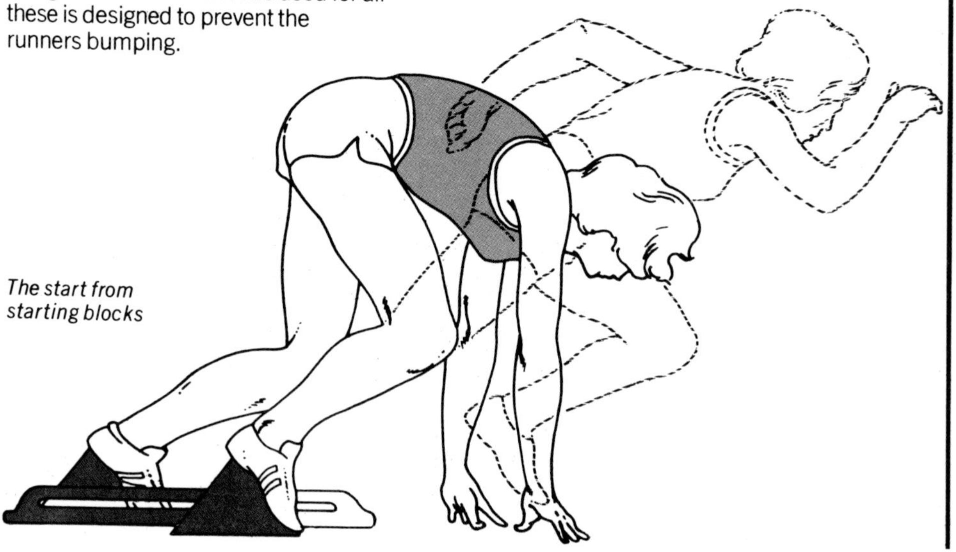

The start from starting blocks

Hurdles

There are 3 different hurdle races; the 110m for men, the 100m for women, and the 400m for both sexes.

Both the shorter distances are run on the straight part of the track. In all events the athletes must remain in their lane. An athlete is not penalised for knocking down a hurdle, but it is not to his or her advantage to knock it down rather than clear it.

In all 4 hurdle events the athletes have to negotiate 10 hurdles. In the men's 110m race the hurdles are 106.7cm (3ft 6in) high and spaced 9.14m (10yd) apart. The women's sprint hurdles are 84cm (2ft 9in) high and spaced 8.5m (9.3yd) apart. In both 400m events the hurdles are 35m (38.28yd) apart and the men's hurdle is 91.4cm (3ft) high while the women's is 76.2cm (2ft 6in).

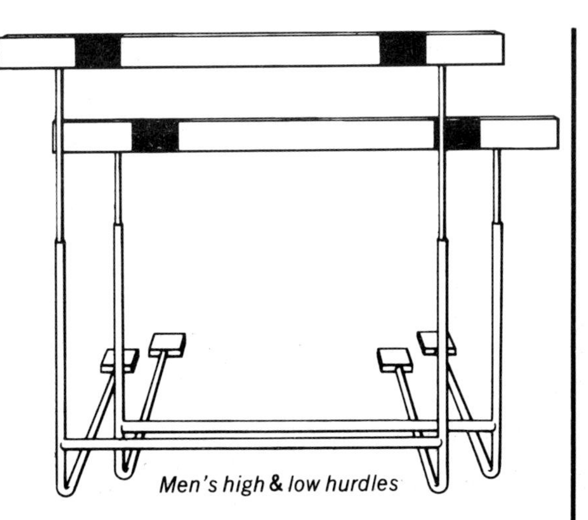

Men's high & low hurdles

Steeplechase

The steeplechase is run over 3000m on a conventional 400m track which is shortened at one end to accommodate the water jump which is normally inside the perimeter of the track. Five obstacles are placed on the track and consist of the water jump and four other barriers. The race starts in the back straight and the runners do not negotiate any barriers until they pass the finish line for the first time. Thereafter they have to negotiate 28 hurdles (4 on each lap), and 7 water jumps. The barriers are 91.4cm (3ft) high and must have a total width of 3.66m (13ft). The water jump is 3.66m (13ft) in width and length and is 70cm (2ft 3½in) deep at the hurdle end, sloping to track level at the other end.

Runners may clear the hurdle without touching it, or by resting one foot on the top of it before making the clearance.

Steeplechase hurdle

Walking

Walking events can take place either on the track or on the open road. The recognised championship distances are 20km and 50km.

For a walking action to be legal, the walker must take steps in such a way that contact with the ground is not broken. In other words, the advancing foot must make contact with the ground before the rear foot leaves it. During the period of each step, while the foot is on the ground, the leg must be straightened (not bent at the knee) at least for 'one moment'.

Contact with the ground must not be broken

Relays

While relay races can be over any distance, like 4 x 1 Mile, the championship distances are 4 x 100m and 4 x 400m. In each case 4 team members have to cover the prescribed distance in the quickest time, running in turn and passing a baton between them by hand.

The baton is round, smooth and hollow, between 28-30cm (11in-12in) long and with a circumference of about 12½cm (5in). It must weigh not less than 50g (1¾oz).

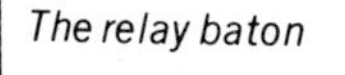

The relay baton

11-12in (28-30cm)

12½cm (5in)

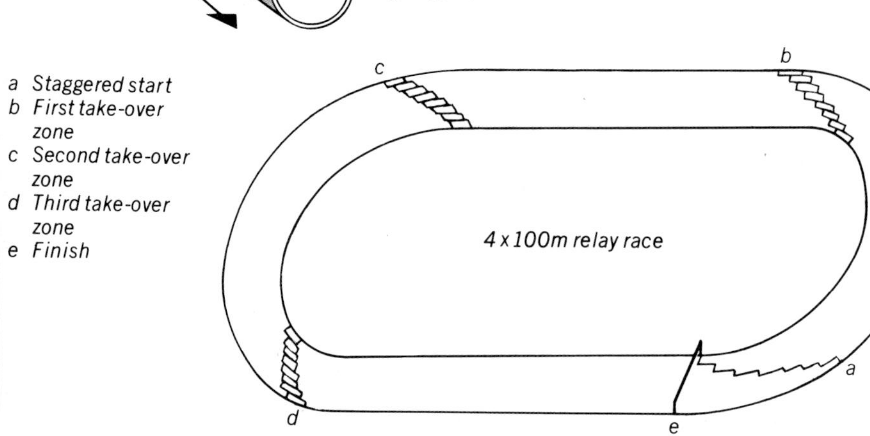

In the shorter relay, known as the sprint relay, each lane has 3 takeover zones marked around the track. Runners must stay in lane, and must make the successful handover in that zone or they are disqualified. In the longer race, the 4 x 400m, the 1st runners complete the opening lap in lane and hand over to the 2nd runners who stay in lane for 100m. Then all runners can break for an inside position. After that the change over is a 'free-for-all' on the start line with the runner from the leading team normally taking up the most advantageous position on the inside of the track.

Decathlon and Heptathlon

The decathlon is contested by male athletes and consists of 10 events, while the women's equivalent is the heptathlon, consisting of 7 events. Both are held over 2 days.

The 10 events of the decathlon are, in order:

Day 1: 100m, long jump, shot, high jump, 400m.

Day 2: 110m hurdles, discus, pole vault, javelin, 1500m.

The 7 events of the heptathlon are, in order:

Day 1: 100m hurdles, high jump, shot, 200m.

Day 2: long jump, javelin, 800m.

Points are awarded for performances in each event, and the winner is the athlete with the most points at the end of the 10, or 7, events.

In the long jump and throwing events, 3 attempts only are allowed and in the running and hurdle races, 3 false starts result in disqualification. An athlete failing to register a score is allowed to stay in the competition, but an athlete failing to start one of the disciplines is not allowed back into the competition.

The current Decathlon and Heptathlon world records

Daley Thompson's Decathlon world record at Los Angeles 8-9 August 1984

Event	Time/dist	Points
100m	10.44 secs	948
Long jump	8.01m (26ft 3½in)	1022
Shot put	15.72m (51ft 7in)	831
High jump	2.03m (6ft 8in)	882
400m	46.97 secs	950
		4633
110m hurdles	14.33 secs*	923
Discus	46.56m (152ft 9in)	810
Pole vault	5.00m (16ft 4¾in)	1052
Javelin	65.24m (214ft 0in)	824
1500m	4:35.00	556
		8798

*time given originally as 14.34 secs, worth 922 points

Sabine Paetz's Heptathlon world record at Potsdam 5-6 May 1984

Event	Time/dist	Points
100m hurdles	12.64 secs	1056
High jump	1.80m (5ft 10¾in)	1031
Shot put	15.37m (50ft 5¼in)	915
200m	23.37 secs	999
Long jump	6.86m (22ft 6¼in)	1089
Javelin	44.62m (146ft 5in)	836
800m	2:08.93	941
		6867

Best ever marks by Sabine Paetz

Event	Time/dist	Points
100m hurdles	12.54 secs	1071
High jump	1.83m (6ft 0in)	1059
Shot put	16.16m (53ft 0¼in)	958
200m	23.37 secs	999
Long jump	7.12m (23ft 4½in)	1141
Javelin	44.62m (146ft 5in)	836
800m	2:07.03	969
		7033

Running shorts and vests need to be of smooth, lightweight materials. Polyester and cotton are the most popular. Rougher materials can cause chaffing. For longer distance running, the vest needs some perforation to allow the escape of excess body heat. Shorts are usually cut-away at the thigh to allow an unrestricted leg movement and, for men, contain a snug-fitting inner skin.

Track suits can vary enormously in price, sometimes simply because they carry a fashionable label. The essential guide is that they are warm, comfortable and easy to slip on and off. This means the trouser legs should be zippered or elasticated at the ankles so they slide simply over running spikes and trainers. For wet weather running, a lightweight, shower-proof jacket is desirable (see inset).

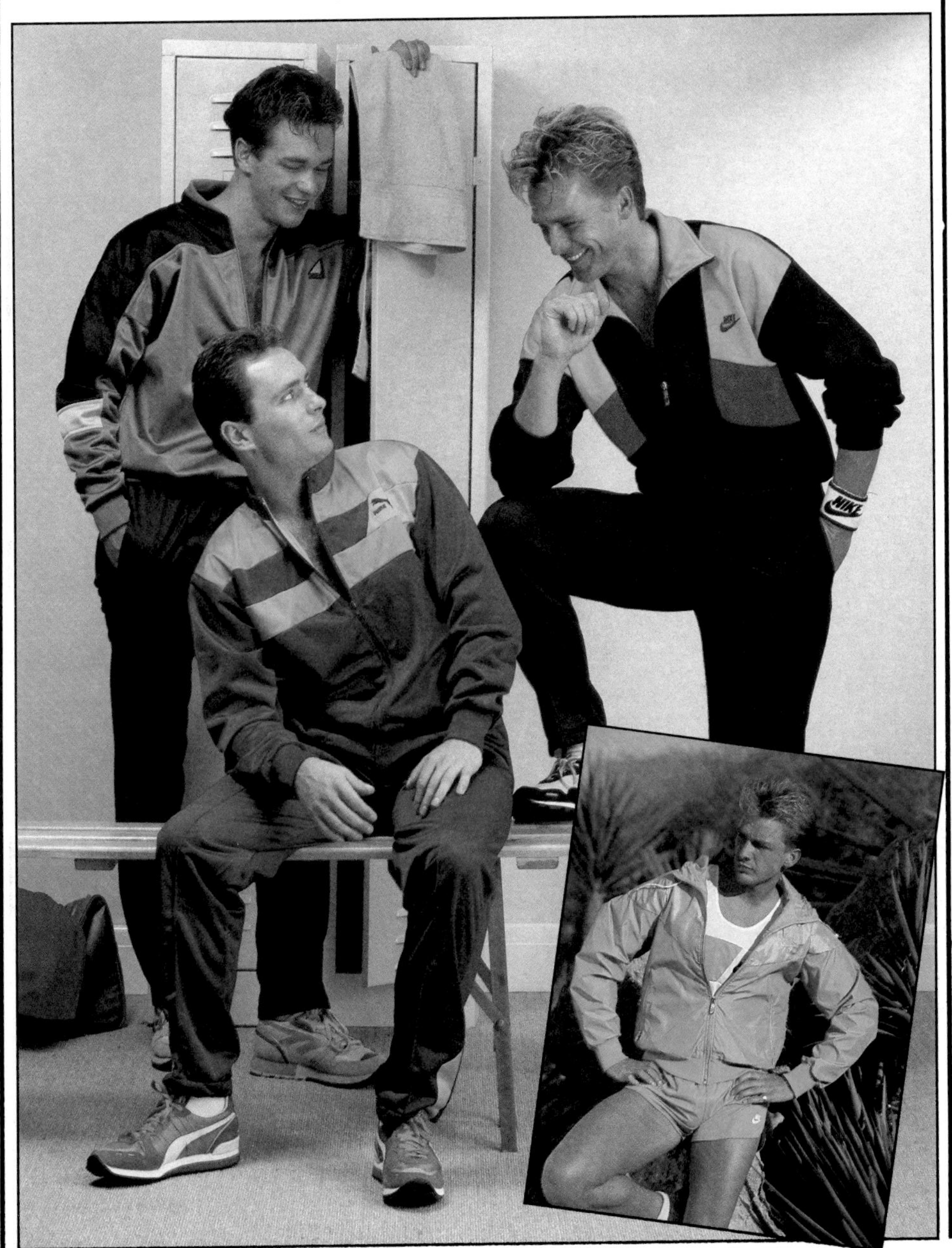

Few areas of sport have undergone such a revolution as the improvement in training shoes. Coinciding with the great jogging/marathon running boom, it has supplied a range of superb footwear that would have ensured that even the great Abebe Bikila did not need to run barefooted in his first Olympic marathon triumph. The major breakthroughs have been:-

(1) the introduction of nylon uppers, replacing the tough, unyielding leather of old;

(2) heavily-cushioned midsoles which protect the feet, legs and lower back during high mileage training, and,

(3) the invention of the waffle sole, which improves shock absorption and traction.

Shoes have also been modified to suit all types of runners: those who land on their heels, those who pronate (that is, rock onto the inside edge of their foot on each landing stride). They also cater for flat-feet, high arches, the swift and the more sedate. There is a shoe now for everyone . . . you just need the patience to find it.

Shot

The men's shot weighs 7.26kg (16lb) and the women's 4kg (8.8lb). The idea is to push (or putt) it from the shoulder as far as possible using just one hand. It must not be thrown. Each putter has 3 throws and the best 8 competitors have 3 more throws each. The putt is made from a circle which is 2.13m (7ft) diameter. At the front edge of the circle is a stop board and a throw is judged a foul if the thrower places a foot on top of the stop board, on top of the circle, or out of the circle.

Hammer Throw

Men only contest the hammer event, attempting to throw the 7.26kg (16lb) weight as far as possible. A spring steel wire attaching the ball to the handle allows the thrower to build up momentum of swing before releasing the hammer. The overall length of the hammer is approximately 1.19m (3ft 11in). Because of the danger of the hammer being released at the wrong time, the throwing circle is protected by a 3.35m (11ft) high cage. Like the shot, each competitor has 3 throws with the best 8 having 3 more attempts.

Discus

Made of wood with a smooth metal rim, the men's discus has a diameter of 220mm (8.6in) and weighs 2kg (4.4lb). The women's discus is 180mm (7in) in diameter and 1kg (2.2lb) in weight. The object of the discus is, again, to throw it as far as possible.

The throw is made from a circle with a 2.5m (8ft $2\frac{1}{2}$in) diameter, and rules governing no-throws are the same as the shot.

Javelin

The javelin is the throwing event in which the greatest distance can be achieved, over 100m (330ft). The men's javelin, made of metal, is 2.7m (8ft $10\frac{1}{4}$in) long and weighs 800g ($1\frac{3}{4}$lb). The women's javelin is 2.3m (7ft 6in) long and weighs 600g ($1\frac{1}{4}$lb). Because of the vast distances it can be thrown these days, the centre of gravity of the men's javelin has been moved in order to reduce the throwing distance. After taking a run-up the thrower releases the javelin from above shoulder height and the javelin must land tip first.

The measurement is taken from the centre of the throwing line to the first point of acceptable landing. If a thrower crosses the throwing line with his foot it is a no-throw.

After 3 throws the leading 8 competitors have 3 more throws.

The men's discus is exactly double the weight of the women's.

The men's shot 7.26kg (16lb) compared to the women's shot of 4kg (8·8 lb) and a tennis ball.

The men's javelin is 40 centimetres longer than the women's and weighs 200 grams more.

High Jump

The winning competitor in the high jump is the one who clears the bar at the greatest height. Or, if 2 or more successfully negotiate the same greatest height, then the one with the fewest jumps at the winning height is the winner. If a tie still occurs the competitor with the least number of failures throughout the competition is the winner. A competitor can elect to join the competition at whatever height he chooses and is allowed 3 attempts to clear the height. However, if he fails to clear a height at the 1st attempt , he can waive his 2 other jumps until the next height. Three successive failures, irrespective of the height, result in elimination.

For a jump to be legal the lift off from the ground must be made by 1 foot, not 2.

The width between the two posts supporting the bar should be between 3.66m-4.04m (12-13ft 3in). The athletes land on a safe bed of foam rubber.

Fosbury Flop

Long Jump

Each competitor has 3 jumps, and the leading 8 then go on for a further 3 jumps, with the one covering the greatest distance in a single jump the winner. In the event of a tie the one with the greatest 2nd best jump is the winner, and so on.

The distance of the jump is measured at right angles from the take-off board to the nearest mark to it made in the sand landing pit by the competitor, no matter which part of his body it was made with. A strip of plasticine is placed in front of the take off board to indicate if an athlete's foot was over the edge of the board. If it was, the jump is declared a 'no-jump'. A competitor who walks back through the landing area after completing his jump is also credited with a 'no-jump'.

There is no restriction to the length of the runway, but it is approximately 1.21m (4ft) wide. The landing area must be a minimum of 2.75m (9ft) wide and 10m (32ft9in) long.

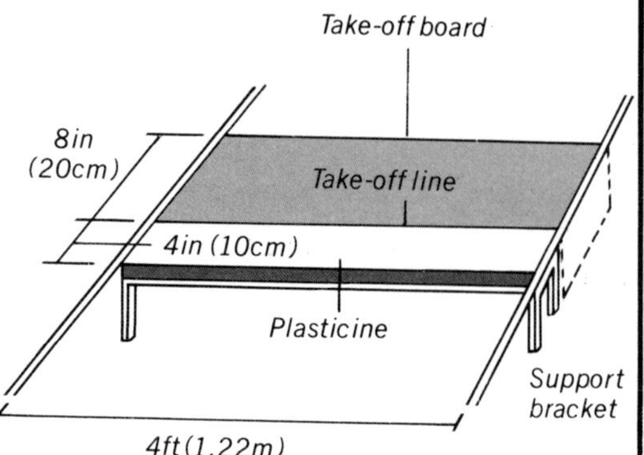

Triple Jump

The triple jump takes place on the same runway as the long jump and competitors have to land in the same landing area. The only difference is that the take-off board is moved further up the runway, and is placed 12.19m (40ft) from the edge of the landing area.

The competitor takes off on one foot. He must then hop on to the same foot, take a step on to the other foot and then complete the jump. The rules governing 'no-jumps' and measuring of distances are the same as the long jump.

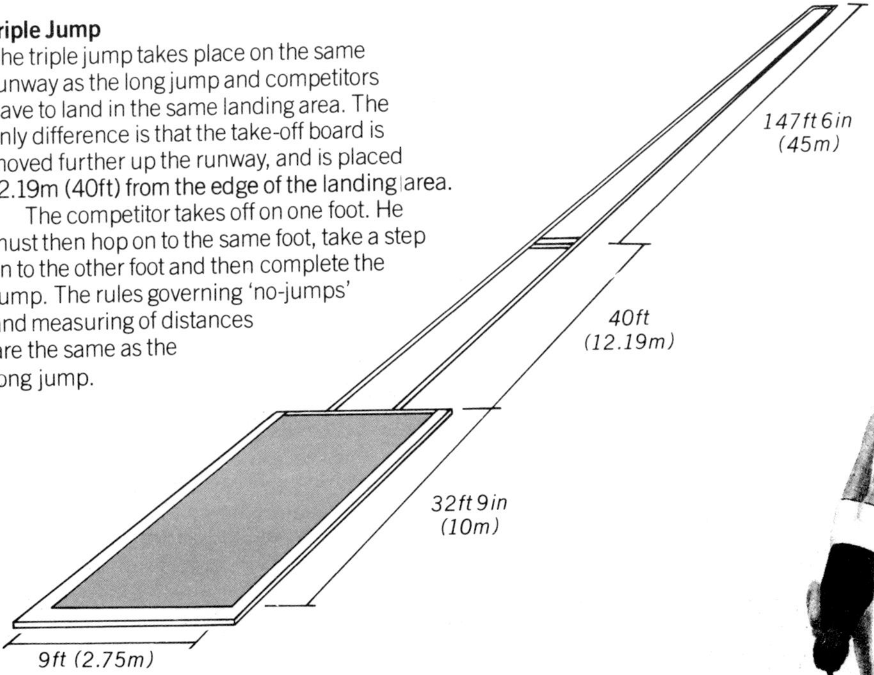

147ft 6in (45m)

40ft (12.19m)

32ft 9in (10m)

9ft (2.75m)

Pole Vault

The principle of the competition and rules governing heights at which competitors may enter competition are the same as the high jump.

The uprights which support the bar are 3.66m-4.37m (12ft-14ft) apart, and the vaulter has to clear the bar with the aid of a flexible pole, usually fibre glass. After his run-up down the runway, the pole is placed in a box directly underneath the bar and by raising his body upwards, the vaulter attempts to clear the bar.

If he does not do so, it is a failure. It is also a failure if the competitor, after leaving the ground, places his lower hand above his upper hand, or moves the upper hand higher on the pole.

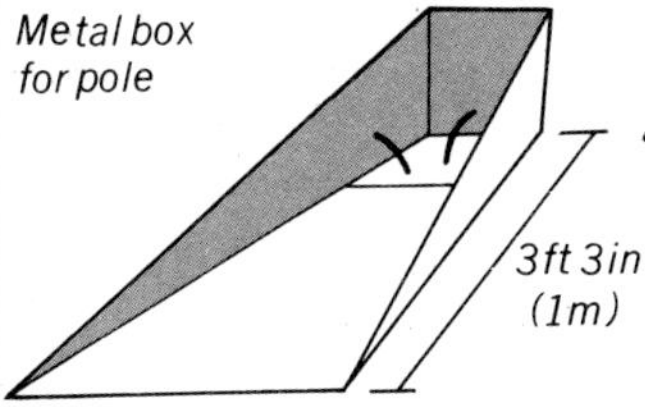

Metal box for pole

3ft 3in (1m)

Badminton

A court game for either 2 or 4 players in singles or doubles. It is a volleying game involving a racket and shuttlecock.

Object
To score more points than your opponent(s) by making successful winning shots.

Duration
A match consists of 3 games, the first person reaching 15 points (11 in ladies' singles) is the winner of each game. The first person to win 2 games wins the match. The laws do permit games to go to 21 points, but this is rarely used in top class competition.

Players
Badminton is generally played as singles, men's doubles, ladies' doubles and mixed doubles.

Shuttlecock

The fragile shuttlecock has 16 goose feathers set in a domed cork base covered in white leather. A small lead weight is set into the base to make the shuttle fly freely. The shuttlecock weighs approximately 1 /10th of an ounce. Because of its delicate nature it is frequently damaged during a game and can be replaced at any time. Shuttles are graded according to weight for use in varying atmospheric conditions.

Racket

Badminton is basically a wrist-action game, so the racket is very light. Most have a metal frame with a steel or carbon fibre shaft though there is an increasing use of graphite. The racket is 26in (66.0cm) long and the head is 8in (20.3cm) wide and covered with tight, natural gut, or synthetic string consisting of about 16 strands horizontal and vertical. Present day rackets weigh around 4oz (113.4g).

Officials
The sole arbiter is an umpire who is responsible for making decisions about the validity of shots, and keeping score. He calls the serving side's score first.

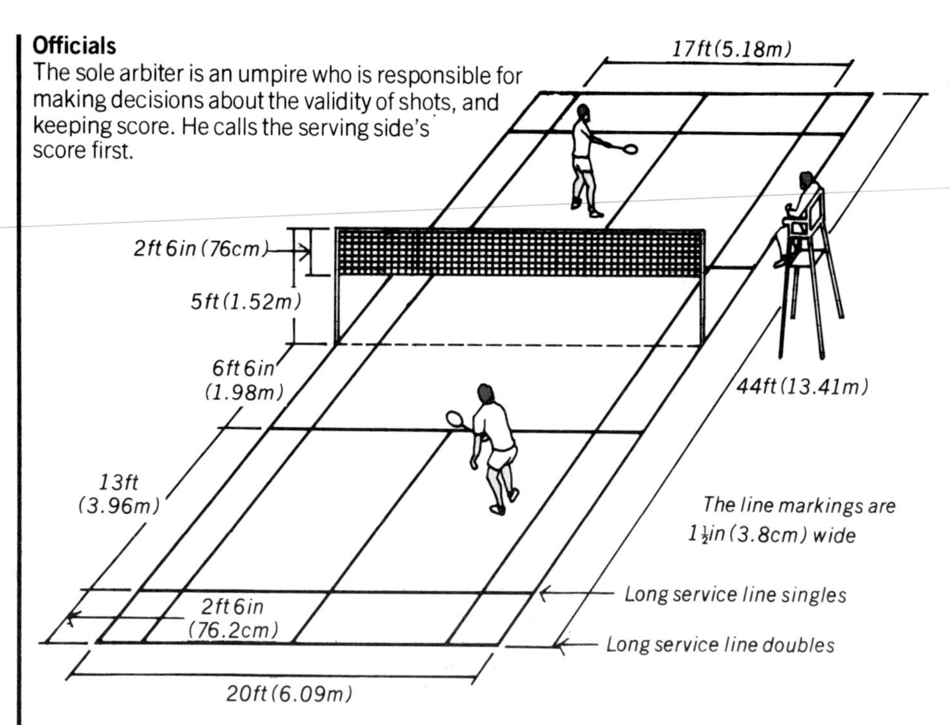

Playing Area
Normally a wooden surface, the court is 44ft (13.41m) long and 17ft (5.18m) wide for a game of singles and 20ft (6.09m) wide in the case of a doubles match when the 1ft 6in (45.7cm) tramlines at either side are brought into use. For ideal conditions there should be a clearance of 3ft (90.5cm) at either side of the court and 6ft (1.83m) at either end. In addition, an air-space clearance of 25-30ft (7.62-9.14m) above the court should exist. A 2ft 6in (76.2cm) deep net stretches across the court at the centre. The top of the net should be 5ft (1.52m) above the court at the centre, and 5ft 1in (1.55m) at the supporting posts. Each half of the court has 2 marked service areas – a right service court and a left service court. The service courts in a game of singles are 8ft 6in (2.59m) wide by 15ft 6in (4.72m) and 8ft 6in (2.59m) by 13ft (3.96m) in doubles.

Scoring
Only the server can score points by winning a rally. If the non-server(s) win the rally, the scores remain unaltered but they take the service, from which points are scored for any successful rallies.

In a game of men's singles the first to score 15 wins the game, but if the scores reach 13-all, the first player to reach 13 has the right to set the match. This means he can decide to carry on to 15 or elect to set to 5 and play to 18. If the game reaches 14-all the game can also be set – whether 13-all was reached or not – but this time can only be set to 3, in other words, until one player reaches 17. If a player opts not to set at 13-all, he can still set at 14-all if he wishes.

In women's singles the game may be *set to 3* at 9-all or *set to 2* at 10-all.

A rally comes to an end if:
The shuttle hits the surface of the court, lands outside its boundaries, or fails to clear the net.
The shuttle is caught on the racket or hit twice or, in the case of doubles, hit simultaneously by both players.
A player touches the net.
A player deliberately baulks or obstructs an opponent.
The service is not underhand.
The receiver allows the service to drop on the court and it lands outside the correct service court.

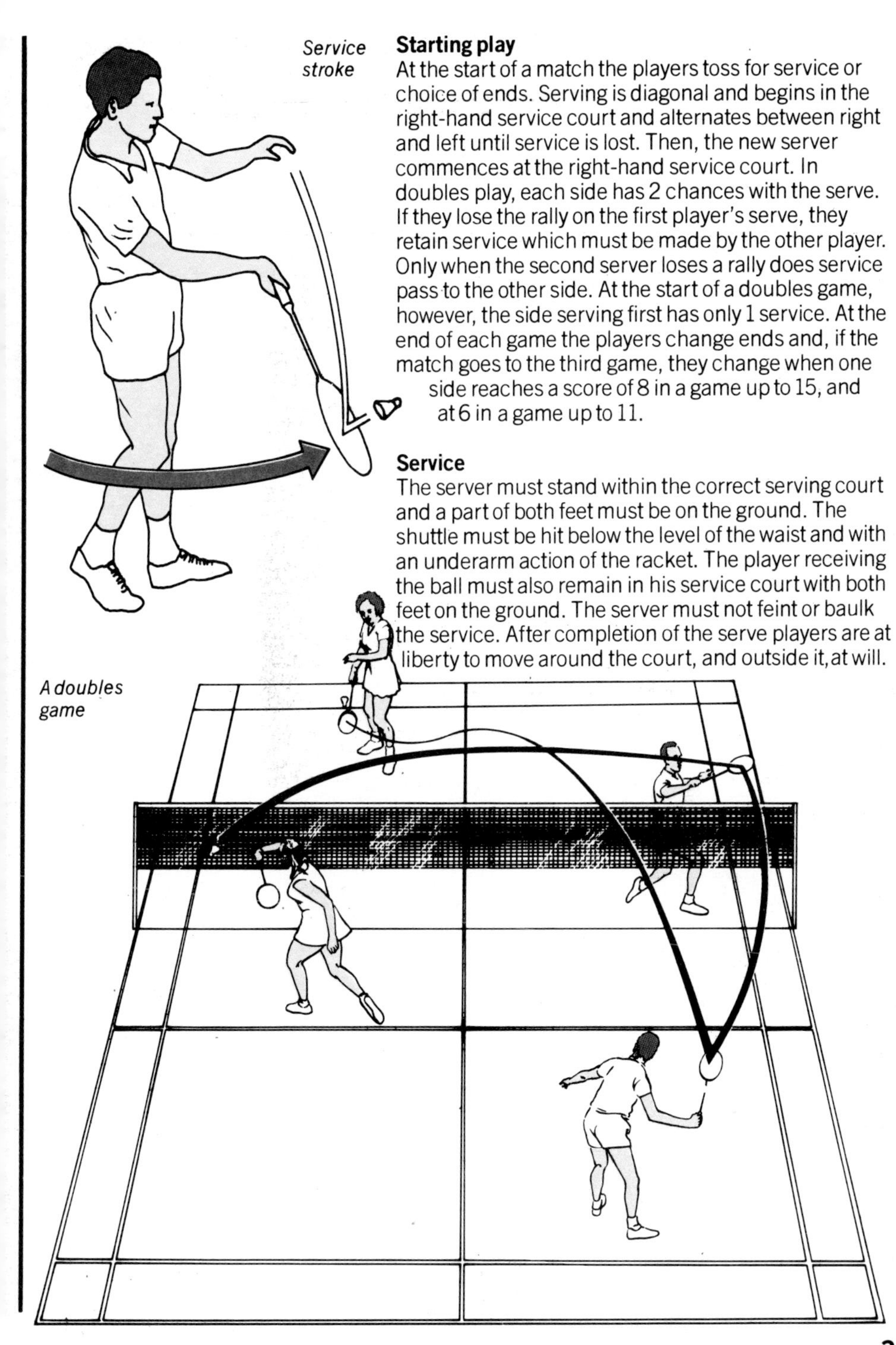

Service stroke

Starting play

At the start of a match the players toss for service or choice of ends. Serving is diagonal and begins in the right-hand service court and alternates between right and left until service is lost. Then, the new server commences at the right-hand service court. In doubles play, each side has 2 chances with the serve. If they lose the rally on the first player's serve, they retain service which must be made by the other player. Only when the second server loses a rally does service pass to the other side. At the start of a doubles game, however, the side serving first has only 1 service. At the end of each game the players change ends and, if the match goes to the third game, they change when one side reaches a score of 8 in a game up to 15, and at 6 in a game up to 11.

Service

The server must stand within the correct serving court and a part of both feet must be on the ground. The shuttle must be hit below the level of the waist and with an underarm action of the racket. The player receiving the ball must also remain in his service court with both feet on the ground. The server must not feint or baulk the service. After completion of the serve players are at liberty to move around the court, and outside it, at will.

A doubles game

Clothing

Badminton is played entirely in white clothing. Men wear white shorts, shirts and socks while women have the choice between shorts or skirts. Both wear rubber or crêpe soled shoes with no heel.

Badminton rackets are very whippy and usually made of steel or graphite. They are strung tightly with about 16 strands of thin gut or synthetic string running horizontally and vertically.

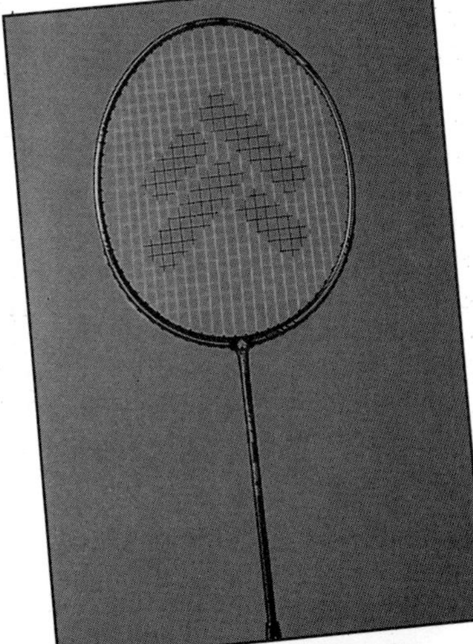

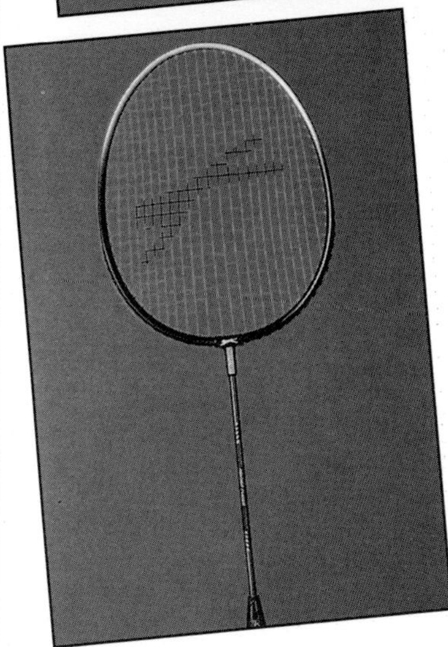

Shuttlecocks are made of feathers or nylon. If feathers, 16 from a white goose are used and fastened with thread. The nylon shuttle is made in one piece and the feathered area is called the skirt.

Baseball

Baseball is a bat and ball game played by 2 teams, each with 9 players. The game, in a different form, was first played in the 18th century and evolved from the English game of rounders. Baseball is the American national sport. The first rules were drawn up in 1845 and the first match under these rules was the following year between the New York Base Ball Club and the New York Knickerbockers (the first organized team).

Object

To score more runs than the opposing side. Each team has 9 innings in which to accumulate runs and the team with the most runs at the end of the match is the winning team.

Duration

There is no fixed time limit. Play continues until both sides have completed their 9 innings. If the scores are level, extra innings are played to determine the winners.

Teams
Teams consist of 9 players with substitutes allowed. Once a player has been substituted, however, he may not take any further part in the game. The positions occupied by the 9 team members are as follows: pitcher, catcher, 1st baseman, 2nd baseman, 3rd baseman, short stop, right fielder, left fielder and centre fielder.

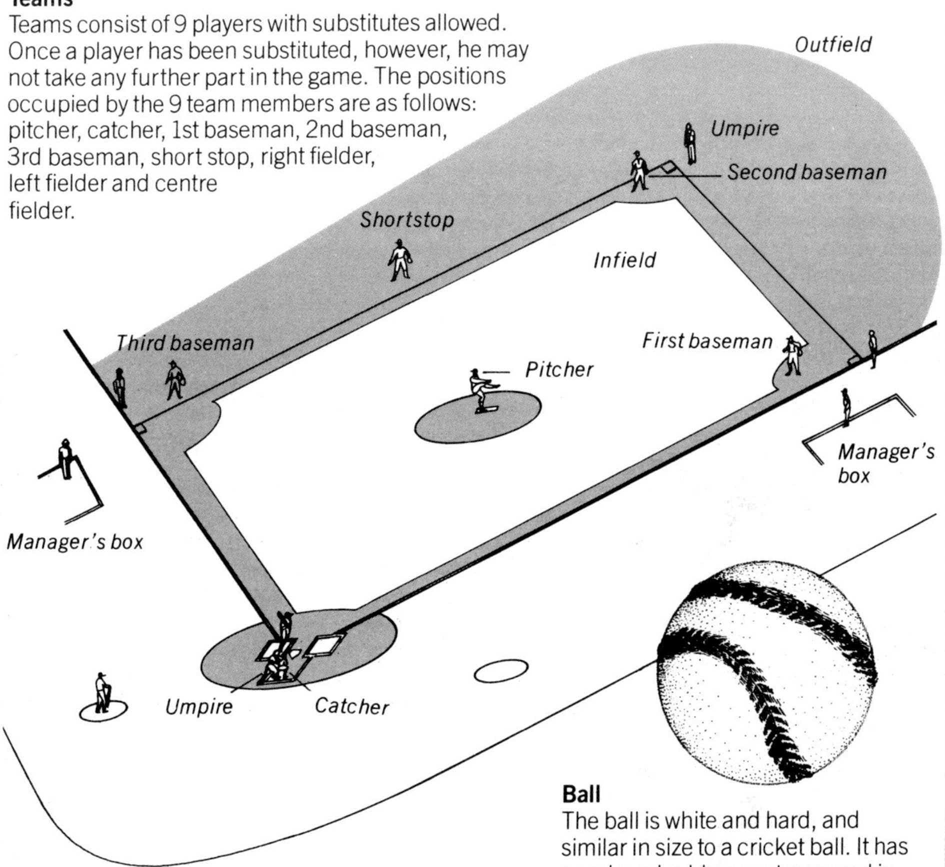

Ball
The ball is white and hard, and similar in size to a cricket ball. It has a cork and rubber centre wound in twine and encased in leather or hide. Its circumference is $9\text{-}9\frac{1}{4}$in (22.5 – 23.5cm) and its weight $5 - 5\frac{1}{4}$oz (142 – 149g).

Officials
A game of baseball is controlled by 4 umpires. 3 stand by bases number 1, 2 and 3, and their main function is to make sure a player reaches the base successfully. The other umpire has the most onerous task of all 4 officials. He stands directly behind the catcher, in line of fire of the ball. His main duty is to make sure the pitcher throws a good ball and, like the catcher, wears protection to his face and chest.

Bat
The bat is made of wood, usually ash. It is smooth and tapers towards the handle. The diameter at the widest part must not exceed $2\frac{3}{4}$in (7cm) and its overall length should not be longer than 42in (1.07m)

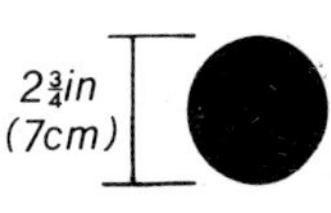

42in (1.07m)

Playing Area

Baseball can be played on grass, but artificial surfaces are more popular these days. A baseball field consists of 2 distinct areas, the infield and the outfield. The infield, commonly known as the diamond because of its shape, is 90ft (27.43m) square. There is no specification to the size of the outfield, except that the boundary fence should be a minimum of 250ft (76.2m) from the apex of the diamond. At each corner of the diamond are bases – 1st, 2nd, 3rd and home. Each of the first 3 bases are indicated by a canvas bag, 15in (38.1cm) square, anchored to the ground. The home base is a 5-sided rubber plate. Straight white lines join the bases to each other. An extension of the lines from home base to 1st base, and home base to 3rd base is marked, and stretches to the boundary fence of the field. The former is known as the right-field foul line, and the latter the left-field foul line. Any ball hit within those lines is in fair territory, but outside the lines it is in foul territory.

A 5ft (1.52m) diameter circle is drawn behind, and at either side, of the home base.

4ft (1.22m)

6ft (1.83m)

4ft 3in (1.29m)

18ft (5.48m)

1ft 5in (43cm)

Home plate base

The Pitcher's plate

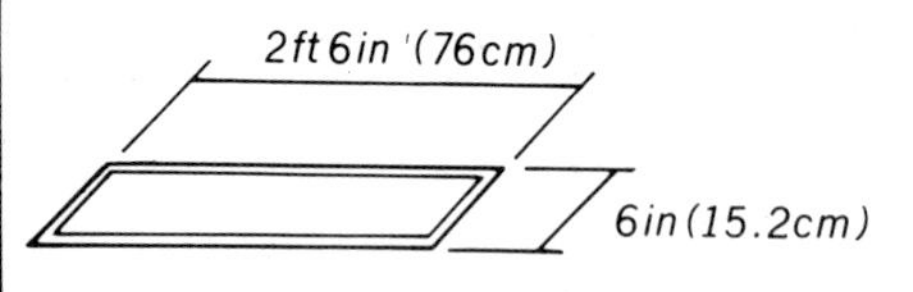

This is called the 'next batter's box' and is where the next batter stands before taking up his batting position.

The pitcher's area, known as the pitcher's plate, is a circle with an 18ft (5.48m) radius and is drawn perpendicular to, and 60ft 6in (18.44m) from the batter's box. Situated within the pitcher's area is the pitcher's mound, approximately 16in (40cm) high, from which the pitcher delivers the ball to the batter.

A 17in (43.2cm) wide plate is marked on the floor of the batter's box – this is called the home plate.

Starting Play

Baseball is unusual in that there is no toss of the coin to decide which side bats first, the visiting team always has that honour.

A game consists of 9 innings. The batter must stand with his bat over the home plate and the pitcher must throw the ball over the plate and between the strike zone, which is between the batter's shoulders and knees when a normal stance is adopted.

If the striker correctly throws the ball and it passes the batter then it is referred to as a *strike*. It is also a strike if the batter swings at the ball and misses, or hits the ball into foul territory. If the pitcher throws the ball high, low, or wide of the strike zone the umpire declares it a *ball*.

If the batter sustains 3 strikes he is out, and the pitcher credited with a strike-out. If the pitcher delivers 4 balls the batter has a free walk to the first base.

Strike zone

The Pitcher – one foot must be in contact with the pitcher's plate

Scoring Runs

Once a batter hits the ball into fair territory, he must drop his bat and run to 1st base. If he feels it safe he may advance further. Any hit which ends with him reaching 1st base is called a single. If he reaches 2nd base it is a double, and a triple if he reaches 3rd base. If he reaches the home base it is a run. It is also a run if he hits the ball out of the playing area, provided it is within the boundary of the fair territory. Once a batter starts his run all team-mates on bases in front of him may run towards the next base. Each one reaching home is credited with a run. If players occupy bases 1, 2 and 3 and, following one hit, all 4 men reach home as a result of that one hit they are said to have completed a Grand Slam Homer.

The batter is out if the ball he hits is caught by a fielder or it falls to the ground and the fielder makes contact with the base towards which the batter is running, before he reaches it. If a ball is caught, all runners must return to the bases they were on before the hit.

A batter must run if he hits the ball into fair territory, consequently the player on 1st base must also run. A player on 2nd base, however, does not have to run on if 1st base is unoccupied. No more than one man at a time is allowed on a base.

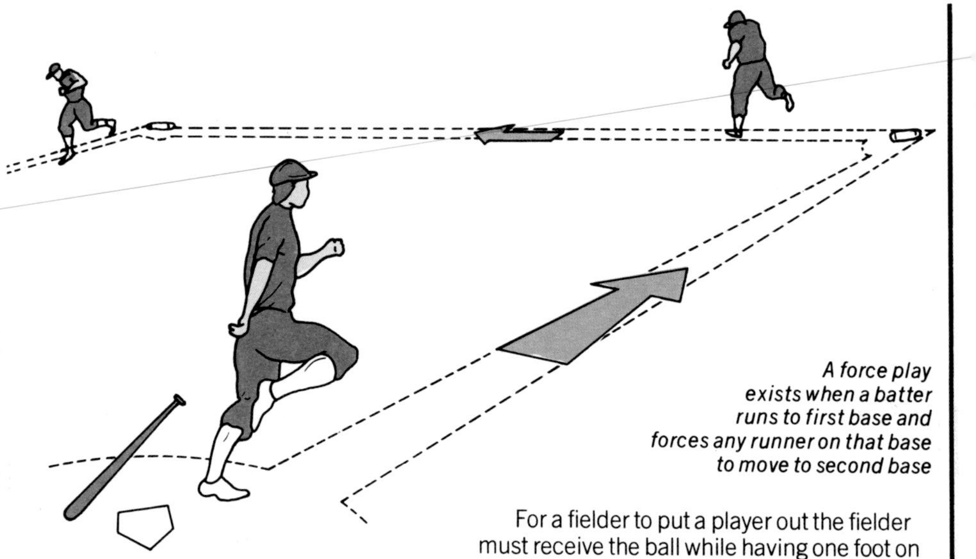

A force play exists when a batter runs to first base and forces any runner on that base to move to second base

For a fielder to put a player out the fielder must receive the ball while having one foot on the base. Alternatively he can 'tag' the player, by touching him with the ball.

Players can 'steal' bases by running from one base to the next when the batter fails to hit the ball, but he can still be put out in the normal way.

The innings (or 'half-innings' as it is called) is ended when 3 batters of one side have been put out. The other team then have their innings (the other 'half-innings'). A team batting second, and leading after the 1st half-innings of the 9th innings does not need to bat again. If all 9 team members have batted and fewer than 3 are out, the players not out may go in to bat again.

A runner is out if a fielder with the ball tags a base before the forced runner reaches base

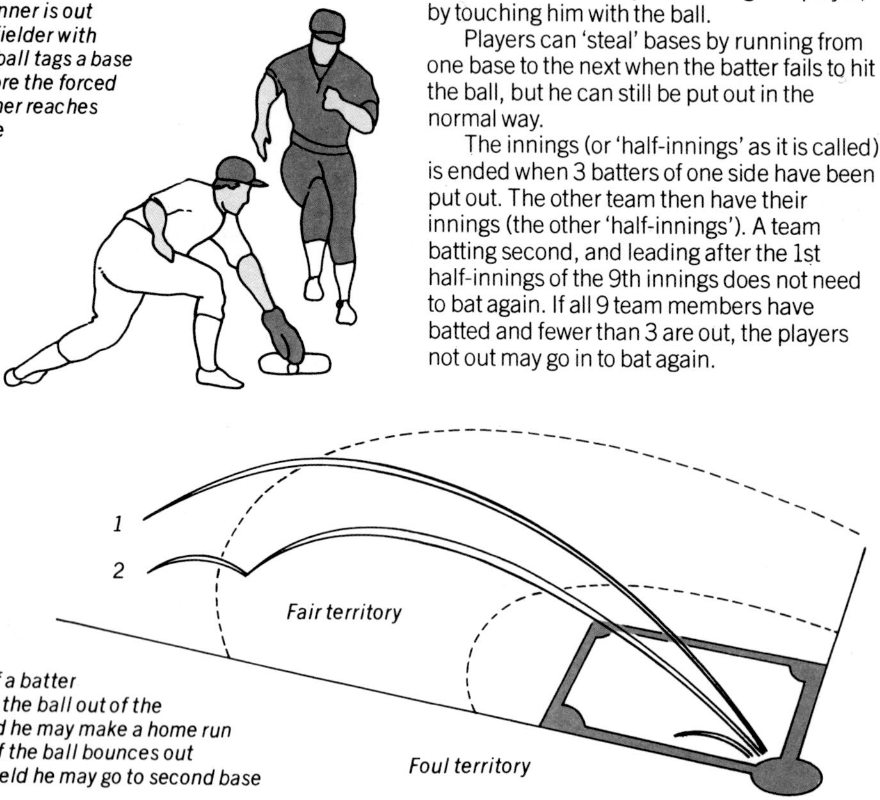

Fair territory

Foul territory

1 If a batter hits the ball out of the field he may make a home run
2 If the ball bounces out of field he may go to second base

Clothing and Equipment

Baseball players have traditionally worn 'plus-four' type trousers with long socks coming to below the knee. They wear shoes with protective steel cleats and, when batting, a protective plastic helmet. It is commonplace for all fielders to wear a glove on their non-throwing hand, i.e. if they are right-handed, the glove is worn on the left hand. The normal glove is made of leather and must be flexible with a webbed pocket to trap the ball.
The catcher, who stands directly behind the batter, wears added protection. His glove is bigger than that worn by the outfielder and is very heavily padded. He also wears a chest protector, shin guards and a metal face mask.

Basketball

Basketball is a ball game played by 2 teams of 5 players, plus up to 7 substitutes each.

Object

To score more points than your opponents by putting the ball in the basket. The points value of a *basket* is either 2 points or 1 point depending on how the scoring shot is made.

Duration

Two halves of 20 minutes each with a 10 minute break in between. Teams swap ends at half-time and, if after the 40 minutes scores are level, a further period of 5 minutes is played. As many extra 5 minute periods as necessary to determine the winners can be played. The clock is stopped as soon as the referee's whistle blows, and is not re-started until play recommences. It also stops for the duration of free throws.

Teams

Each team consists of a centre, 2 forwards and 2 guards. Substitutes may replace another player at any time.

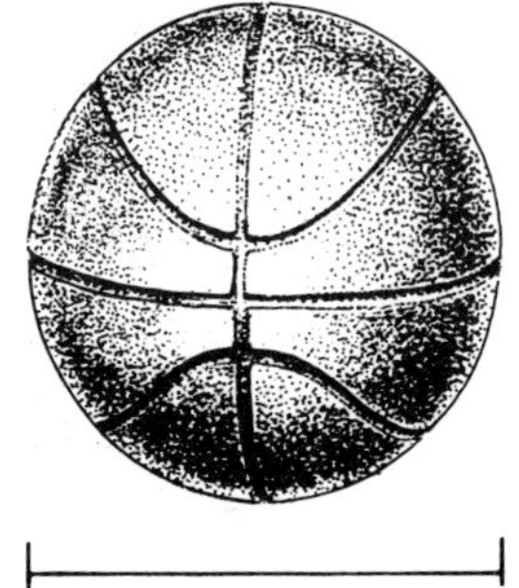

Officials
A game is controlled by a referee and umpire who are on the court simultaneously. Both have equal jurisdiction during the game although ultimate authority on all matters falls to the referee. They are assisted by a time-keeper, scorer and 30-second scorer.

Ball
Made of leather or composition covering, the basketball is round, approximately 30in (75-78cm) in circumference and normally orange coloured. It weighs between 20 and 22oz (60-650gm) and should be inflated to such a pressure that, when dropped from a height of 6ft (1.83m) on a solid wooden floor, it will bounce a little over 4ft (1.20-1.40m).

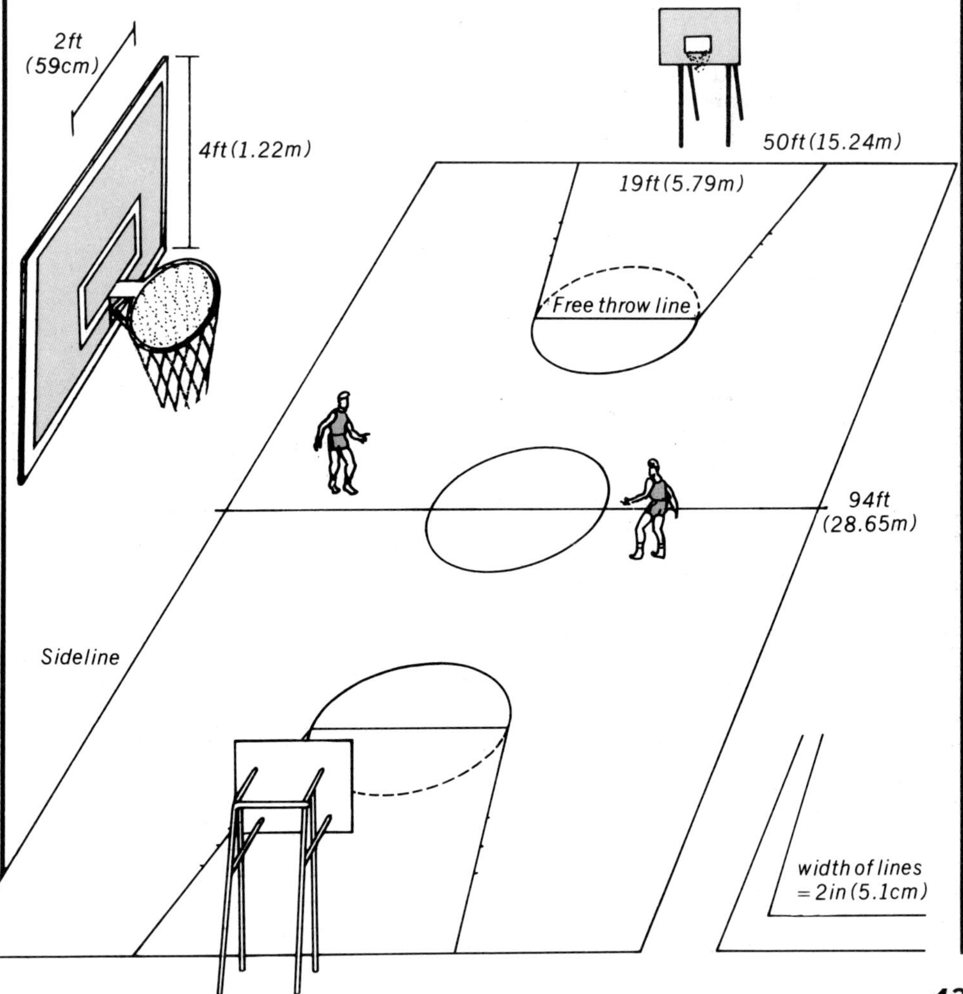

Playing Area

The playing area is rectangular measuring 94ft (28.65m) by 50ft (15.24m). Sidelines and endlines mark the perimeter. These lines are 2in (5.1cm) wide. A division line separates the 2 halves of the playing area and 2 concentric rings are drawn in the middle of the division line – one with a radius of 2ft (61.0cm) and the other with a radius of 6ft (1.83m).

At each end of the court there is a free-throw area marked out. It is rectangular, 12ft (3.66m) wide and extending 19ft (5.79m) from the endline. A semi-circle with a radius of 6ft (1.83m) is added to the free-throw area. That part of the court is known as the key because of its resemblance to a keyhole. No player is allowed to remain in that area for more than 3 seconds while his team has possession of the ball. The distance from the free-throw line to the plane of the backboard holding the net is 15ft (4.57m).

The backboard is made of wood or unbreakable glass and extends 4ft (1.22m) onto the court. The baskets are attached to the backboard and the metal ring which supports the net has an inside diameter of 18in (45.7cm). The net is between 15-18in (38.1 – 45.7cm) in length. The upper edge of each basket is 10ft (3.04m) above and parallel to the floor and must be 6in (15.2cm) from the face of the backboard.

Free throw position

Jump off

Starting Play

The game begins with a jump-off. Two players, one from each team, stand in the centre circle with their feet inside the half of the circle nearer to their own basket. The referee tosses the ball up for those players to compete in an attempt to tap it to a team mate. They must not catch the ball at the jump-off, during which, all other players must be outside the semi-circle.

The intention is to get the ball up field and into the opponents' basket. This can be achieved by passing the ball to a team mate or by dribbling. When dribbling the player must not hold on to the ball for more than a single pace but can proceed forward by bouncing the ball at the same time. Once he catches the ball during a dribble, he cannot start another – he must pass or shoot at goal.

A team can shoot at goal from anywhere on the playing area, but it is obviously advantageous to get as near the basket as possible. They must shoot within 30 seconds of gaining possession of the ball.

If the ball goes through the basket, 2 points are awarded and the side conceding the points start the game from their own endline. If the ball misses the basket and is thrown over the sideline the opposing team restart play with a throw in.

Baskets scored from free throws as a result of an infringement are worth 1 point.

Moving with the ball

A player may pivot on one foot while moving in any direction with the other foot

Infringements

Some personal contact is acceptable, but players are not allowed to hold, barge into, push, or impede the progress of opponents. If such contact takes place the offending player is penalised for committing a *personal foul* and the opposing team awarded a free throw from the free-throw line. If the *personal foul* was committed while the player was attempting a shot at goal, and the shot was unsuccessful, 2 free throws are awarded.

The other form of foul is the *technical foul*. This is for an offence committed against the spirit of the game – deliberate time-wasting, leaving the court without permission or unsporting conduct. Two free throws are again awarded for such a breach, but, if the breach was made by a coach or substitute, then only 1 throw is the penalty.

If a player travels with the ball, does not bounce it while moving forward, or dribbles with 2 hands he is penalised and possession passed to the opposing team.

Any player who commits 5 fouls during the course of a game is automatically sent off. But the referee has a right to dismiss a player at any time if he feels he has blatantly violated the rules. In both cases the dismissed player may be replaced by a substitute.

Interference
A player must not touch the ball in its downward flight above the ring

Personal foul pushing

Personal foul barging

Personal foul charging

Personal foul blocking

Size for numbers on front and back of vests

Time Out
Each coach may call for 2 *time-outs* in each half, and 1 in each extra time period. The time out lasts 1 minute and must be called while the ball is out of play. The purpose of the *time-out* is to give the coach the opportunity to change tactics or deliver a pep talk.

Clothing
Each team wear matching shorts, sleeveless shirts, and socks. The players wear numbers on the front and back of their vests. In international competition, only the numbers 4-15 inclusive are used. Players also wear specially constructed shoes with rubber soles and leather or canvas uppers.

The basketball is made of a leather, rubber or moulded nylon casing around a rubber inner bladder.

Basketball rings are made of solid iron and painted orange. They are rigidly attached to the hardwood backboards and stand 10ft (3.05m) above the floor. The nets are of white cord, 15¾in (40cm) in length, which momentarily check the ball as it passes through.

Basketball footwear is boot-like, with rubber soles and leather or canvas uppers which stretch over the ankles for protection against twists and strains.

Bowls

An indoor or outdoor game played either by individuals, pairs, triples or foursomes. There are 2 forms of bowls, crown green and lawn bowls – also known as flat green bowls. The increasingly popular indoor game is played to the flat green rules. The main difference between the two codes -crown and lawn- is that the playing area for crown bowls does literally have a crown on it, giving an uneven surface, whereas lawn bowls is played on a completely flat surface.

We all know Sir Francis Drake was playing bowls at Plymouth Hoe on July 1588, when the Spanish Armada was sighted. But the history of the game dates back much further – possibly 7000 years.

Implements for a game similar to the current 10 pin bowling were found in the grave of a child believed to have been buried around 5200 B.C. Man has most probably played a form of bowls, by throwing stones or rocks at a target, from the earliest days. Lawn bowling as it is known today certainly dates from the 13th century, and the Southampton Bowls Club organised a tournament on a green in 1299. It became an organised sport in the mid 19th century and the first code of laws were drawn up in 1949. The Scottish Bowling Association was formed in 1892 and the English equivalent followed 11 years later with the legendary cricketer W.G. Grace as its first president. The British Crown Green Bowling Association was founded in 1932.

Object
To roll your bowl or bowls nearer to the jack than your opponent. The number of bowls nearer to the jack than your opponent is the number of points you score on each roll, known as an *end.*

Duration
In singles the game finishes once a player reaches 21 points. In pairs and fours it is played over 21 ends, with an extra end being played if the scores are level. And in triples play a game is over 18 ends. In some crown green games a match can go up to 31, or even 41 points. Televised indoor events have seen a change in the scoring to provide more entertainment, and each match consists of a pre-determined number of sets, usually 5 with the first player reaching 7 points winning each set.

Official
A referee, or marker, decides which ball or balls are nearer the jack. He is also responsible for the accuracy of any measurements taken in cases of dispute and guides the players when they ask for his opinion on the state of play at any time.

Pairings (Lawn Bowls)
In singles, each player delivers 4 bowls, alternating with his opponent. Each player also delivers 4 bowls in pairs, but in triples each delivers 3, while In fours each delivers only 2.

Pairings (Crown Green Bowls)
Singles is the most popular game under crown green rules but, unlike the flat green game, players have only 2 bowls each. Occasionally pairs are played, again with each player having 2 bowls.

The Jack Lawn Bowls

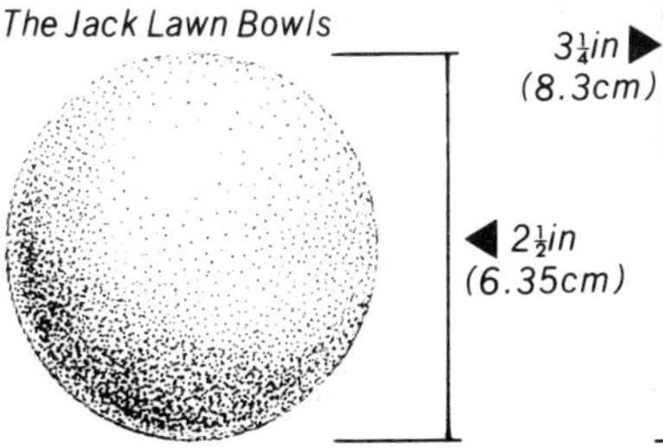

◀ 2½in (6.35cm)

Jack
Players attempt to get their own bowl as near as possible. The jack is smaller than the bowls, 2½in (6.35cm) in diameter, 8-10oz (226.8-283.5g) in weight, and is coloured white.

Bowls
Commonly referred to as 'woods', most modern bowls are, in fact, made of a hardened rubber or lignum vitae. They are either black or brown in colour and, in major competitions, have a colour ring to indentify each player's woods from another. Each lignum vitae bowl must not exceed 16½in (41.9cm) in circumference nor 3½lb (1.59kg) in weight. Wooden bowls must not be loaded with metal weights. Composition bowls, however, vary in size according to different national associations. But, in most cases, vary little from the specifications mentioned above. No actual rules govern the size of bowls in the crown green game, although they are little different from the flat green bowls.

All bowls are flattened on one side. This is known as the 'bias', which causes the bowl to travel in a curved path, rather than a straight line. The amount of bias allowed on a bowl is governed by regulations. Generally, bowls vary between a number 1 bias to a number 5. The number 1 travels relatively straight compared to the number 5.

Crown Green Bowls

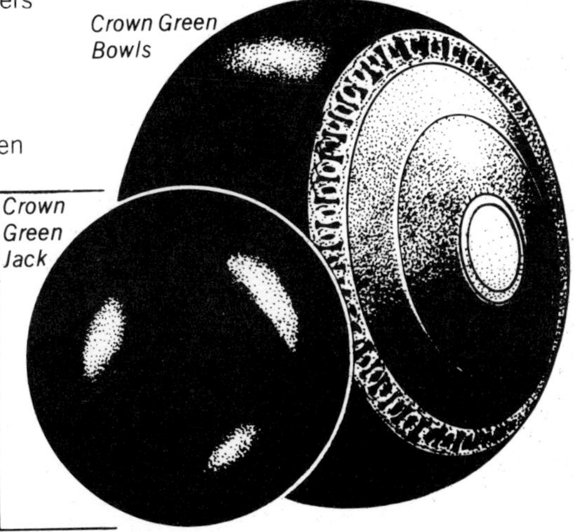

Crown Green Jack

3¼in ▶ (8.3cm)

Playing Area (Lawn Bowls)
The area must be completely flat and either be grass or an approved artificial surface, which is more popular indoors. The normal playing area is 40yd (36.58m) square and surrounded by a 12in (30,48cm) wide x 2in (5.08cm) deep ditch. The playing area is divided into 6 'rinks' each the length of the playing area and between 19-21ft (5.79-6.40m) wide. Play takes place from one end of the rink to the other, and vice versa after each end if completed.

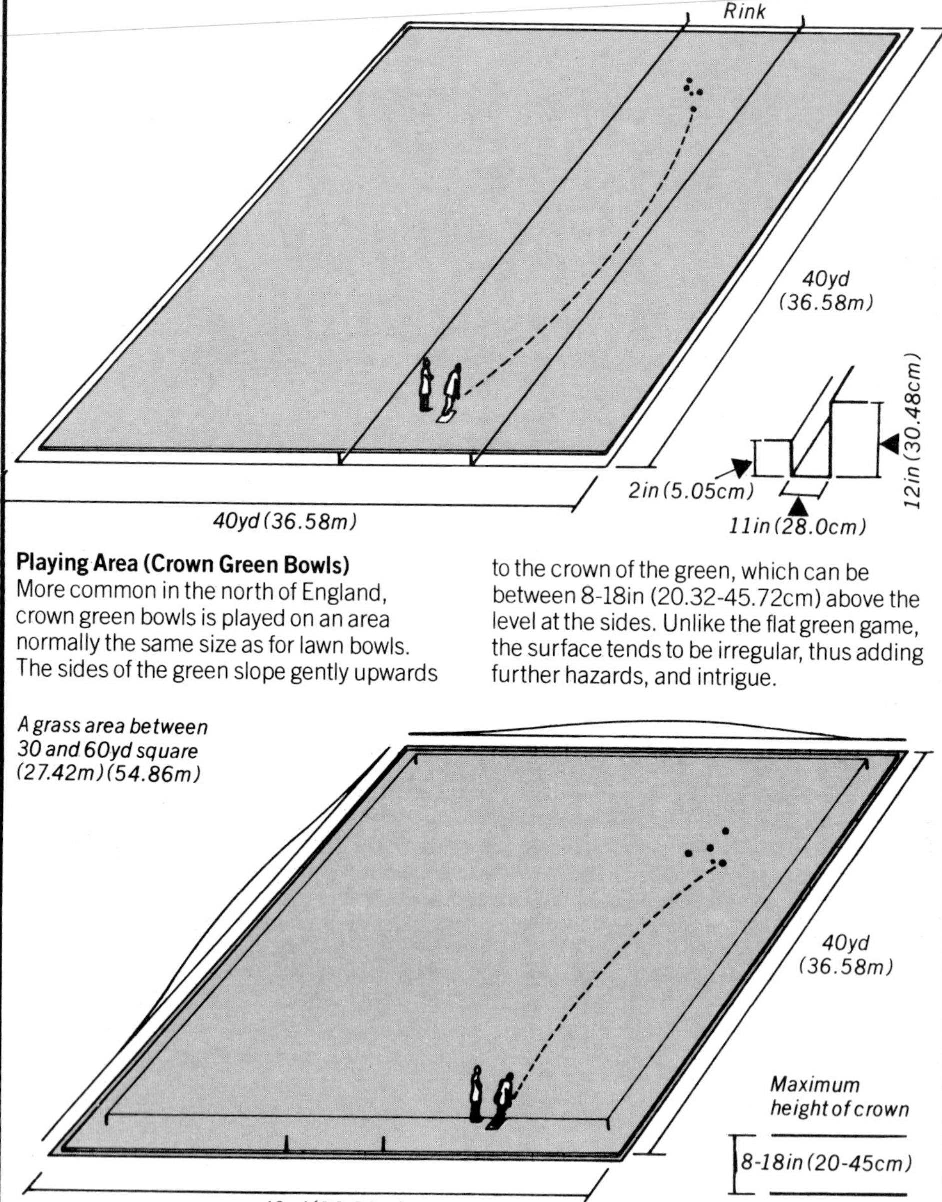

Playing Area (Crown Green Bowls)
More common in the north of England, crown green bowls is played on an area normally the same size as for lawn bowls. The sides of the green slope gently upwards to the crown of the green, which can be between 8-18in (20.32-45.72cm) above the level at the sides. Unlike the flat green game, the surface tends to be irregular, thus adding further hazards, and intrigue.

Starting Play (Lawn Bowls)
A toss of a coin decides which bowler goes first. That player places a rubber mat on the rink. The back of it must be 4ft (1.22m) from the ditch, and it must be placed in the middle of the rink. He must have one foot on this every time he delivers a wood. It must not be moved until the completion of each end. After each end, the winning player has the right to place the mat where he desires providing it is in the centre of the rink, its back edge is 4 feet from the ditch and, its front edge is not less than 27yd (24.69m) from the opposite ditch.

To start a game, the first bowler rolls the jack along the rink at least 25yd (22.86m). An official then centres the jack in the middle. The player who throws the jack correctly plays the first wood, and both players then roll alternately. Once all woods have been bowled the end is over and the player with more bowls nearer the jack than his opponent wins the appropriate number of points.

Any bowl that travels less than 15yd (13.72m) from the mat is 'dead' and is removed from the green. Balls that cross the dividing line marking each rink are also 'dead' and removed, as are balls that enter the ditch without first touching the jack. Any ball that strikes the jack, either directly or as a result of a 'cannon', and enters the ditch, is live, and is a possible end-winning bowl.

Starting Play (Crown Green)
The rubber mat, or *footer,* is circular in crown green bowls, but it serves the same purpose as in lawn bowls. The rules governing its use are slightly different however; a player who throws the jack with his right hand, must throw his wood with the same hand and must have his right toe on the *footer.* The opposite applies to left-handed players.

Start of play is determined by the toss of a coin and the person delivering the first jack must make it travel at least 21yd (19.20m), but he can roll it in any direction – forward, sideways or diagonally. The jack is not deemed 'good' if it travels less than 21yd (19.20m), or comes to rest inside a radius of 3yd (2.74m) of the centre of the green, or if jack and footer are within 4yd (3.66m) from the same edge of the green.

At the finish of each end the winning player has the choice of direction and distance he throws the jack.

In crown green bowls there is always the danger of bowls from one match interfering with those of another because so many matches take place in different directions. Jacks or woods interfered with accidentally can be replayed.

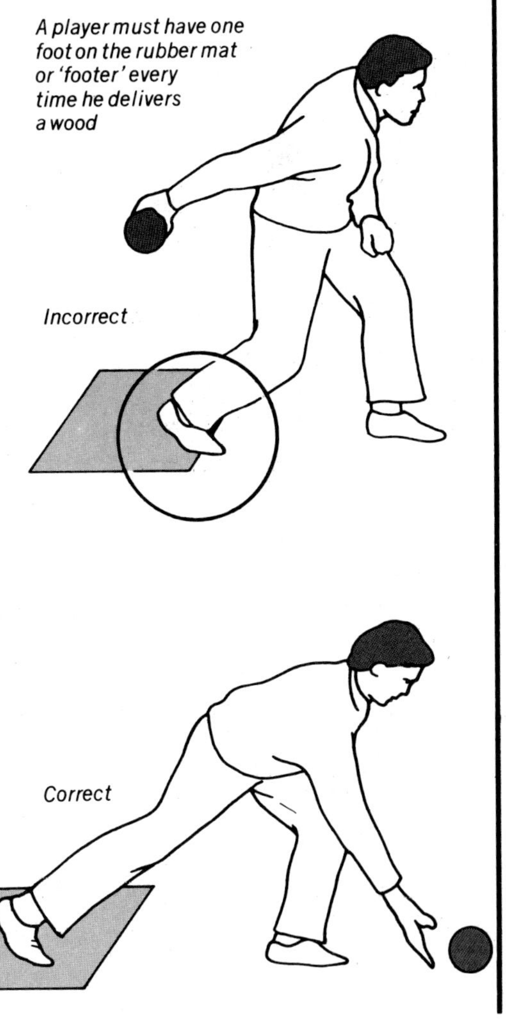

A player must have one foot on the rubber mat or 'footer' every time he delivers a wood

Basic Shots

There are 3 basic shots, the draw, the firing shot and the trail. The draw, involves curling the ball in from right to left towards the jack. In the case of the right-handed player this is known as using the forehand. If he draws from left to right, it is known as the backhand draw. The firing shot is often used when all seems lost and there is no way into the jack. The wood is delivered with pace in the hope of dispersing all balls and salvaging a point, or reducing the opponent's advantage. For the trail shot the wood picks up the jack and travels with it for a few feet before they both come to rest adjacent to each other.

Drawing from the left

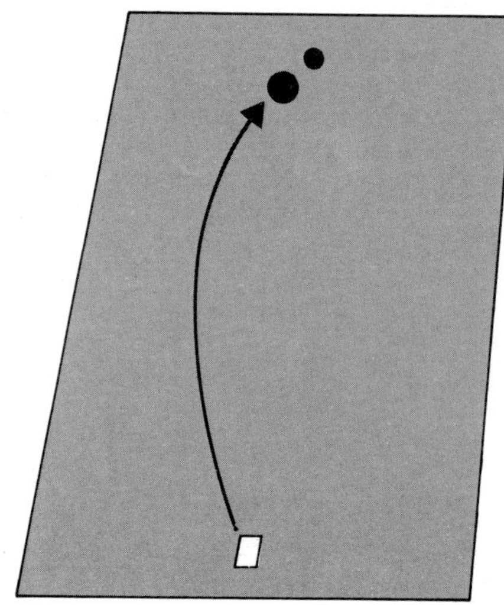

Drawing from the right

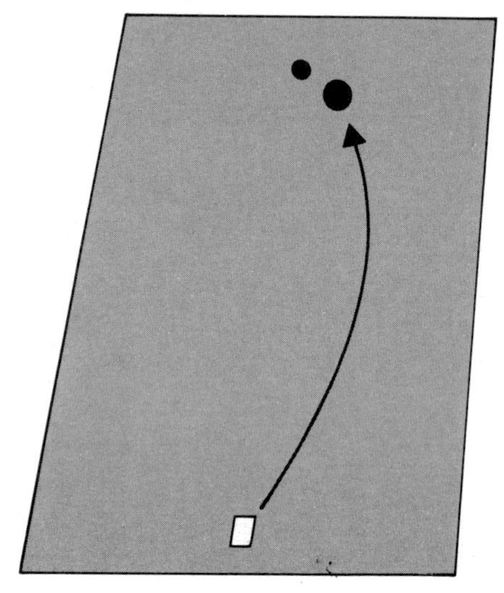

The firing shot

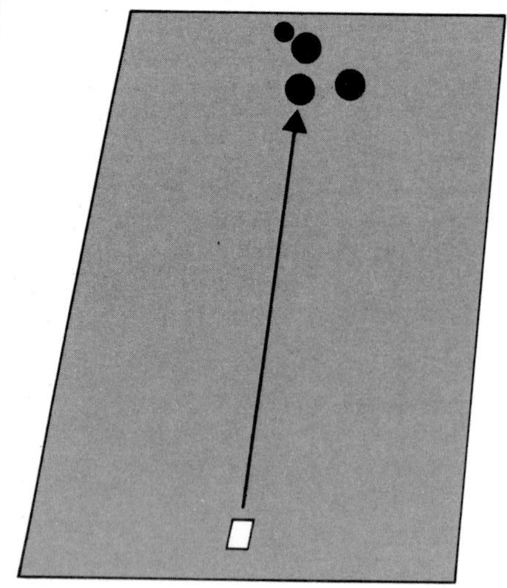

The trail

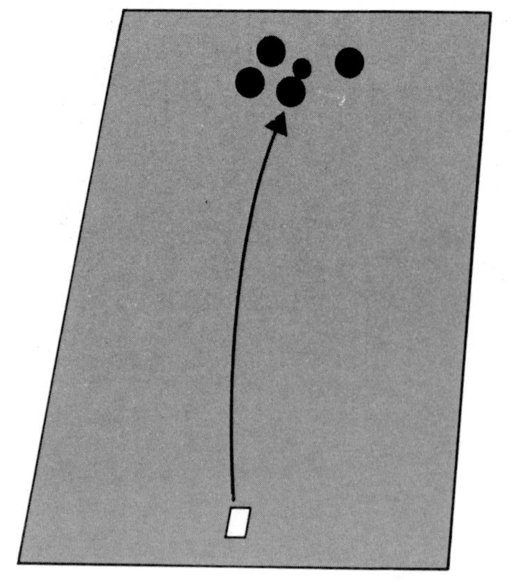

Clothing

The flat green game calls for a more formal approach to dress than does the crown green game. White flannel trousers and white shirt are standard for male players, although wearing of a jacket is a fast-diminishing requisite. Women do, however, still tend to wear jackets with their skirts. All bowlers, no matter what code they play, must wear flat soled shoes so as not to damage the playing surface.

In televised indoor bowls players wear distinguishing shirts, normally red or blue, which match the colour of the identifying marks on their bowls.

Bowls, or "woods" as they are known, are made of composition, hardened rubber or wood (lignum vitae). Metal loading of bowls made of wood is strictly forbidden. They are black or brown.

Cricket

Cricket is a bat and ball game for 2 teams of 11 players. Substitutes are allowed only to replace a fielder, and may not replace a batsman.

The origin of cricket is not known, although it is almost certain to have first been played in England. Edward I made reference to the sport in 1300 and an Elizabethan coroner spoke about playing 'Creckett' at Guildford in 1560. The first known cricket club, Hambledon, was formed in the 1760s and 100 years later the County Championship was introduced, although it did not receive official status until 1890.

Object

To score more runs that the opposing team by either successfully running between the wickets after striking the ball, or hitting the ball to, or over, the boundary fence. The winning team is the one with the most runs.

Duration
A cricket match can last for a pre-determined number of overs, or for a period of time. The former is used in the popular one-day matches which, as the title implies, are scheduled to be completed in one day. But bad weather can cause play to be abandoned and carried over to the next day. Most one-day matches consist of one innings per team.

Matches over a pre-determined period of time can be over 3 days (as in the County Championship) or 5 days (as in Test Matches). In both cases the actual playing time is approximately 6 hours per day, and each team has 2 innings each. There is a 10 minute interval between each innings.

Fielding Positions
(for a right-handed batsman):
1 bowler
2 wicket keeper
3 slips
4 leg slip
5 backward short leg
6 square short leg
7 forward short leg
8 silly point
9 gully
10 silly mid off
11 silly mid on
12 mid wicket
13 square leg
14 backward point
15 point
16 cover
17 short extra cover
18 extra cover
19 deep extra cover
20 mid off
21 deep mid off
22 mid on
23 deep mid on
24 short fine leg
25 deep fine leg
26 short third man
27 third man
28 long leg
29 deep square leg
30 deep mid wicket
31 long on
32 long off

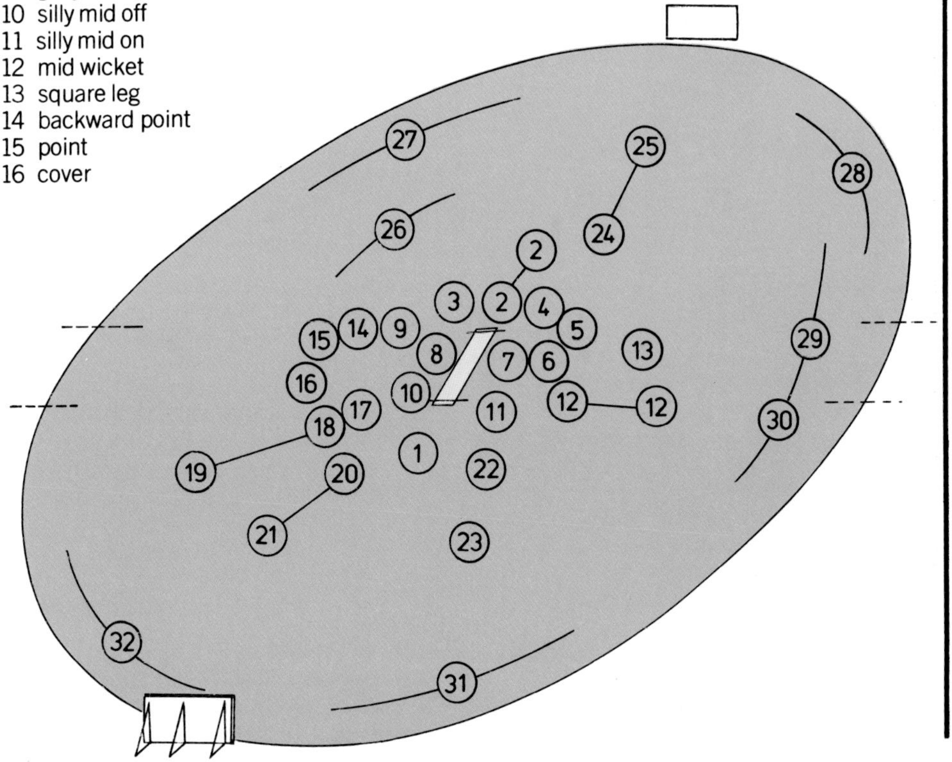

Teams
Each team consists of 11 players. Substitutes are allowed to replace injured fielders. A substitute may not bat or bowl, but he can assist an injured batsman by acting as his runner . . . running between the wickets on his behalf.

Right-hand batsman

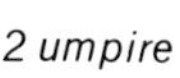

Officials
Two umpires officiate in cricket. One stands at the opposite end to the facing batsman and gives decisions concerning appeals for the batsman's dismissal. He also counts the balls in the over. The other umpire stands level with the batsman but some way to his right or left (depending on which hand the batsman uses). He gives decisions on run-outs and stumpings and watches the bowler's action. At the end of each over, the umpires take up the opposite positions. The umpires indicate to the official scorer how many runs are scored off each ball in boundaries and byes, and the scorer keeps a detailed and accurate record of the proceedings.

1 umpire

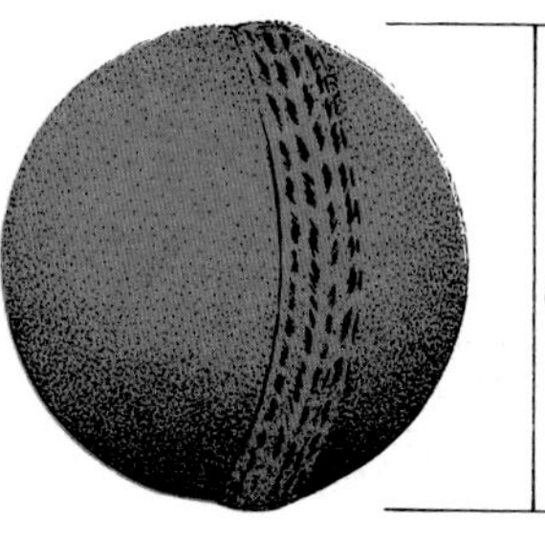

9in (22.9cm)

38in (96.5cm)

Bat
The bat is made of wood, usually willow, flat on one side and rounded on the reverse. It is with the flat side that the batsman attempts to strike the ball. The handle is made from cane and covered in a rubber grip. The blade of the bat is normally coated in a laminated material for protection. Bats vary in size and weight for personal preference but the laws state a maximum overall length of 38in (96.5cm) and a maximum width of $4\frac{1}{4}$in (10.8cm) at the widest part.

Ball
Solid and covered in a shiny leather casing. It weighs not less than $5\frac{1}{2}$oz (155.9gm) or more than $5\frac{3}{4}$oz (163g) and measures not less than 8 13/16in (22.4cm) or more than 9in (22.9cm) in circumference. Because the shine goes from the ball with constant use, captains may demand a new ball at the start of each innings. In matches of 3 or more days, the ball may be changed every 75 overs. The captain of the fielding side decides if he wants to take the new ball. A shiny ball helps fast bowlers with swing, whereas one made rough can help the spinner's grip.

Playing Area

A cricket pitch is normally grass. The actual playing area can be any size and shape, but ideally there should be a minimum of 75yd (68.58m) from the wickets – which should be, as near as possible, in the centre of the playing area – to the boundary fence or line. The wickets are either end of a specially mown stretch of grass known as the strip. It is 22yd (20.12m) long and a minimum 12ft (3.66m) wide. The wickets consist of 3 wooden, cylindrical stumps. They are 28in (71.1cm) high from the ground to the top of them. The width of the 3 stumps when set equidistant apart, is 9in (22.86cm). Two wooden bails are placed into grooves on top of the wickets. In front of each set of wickets is a rectangular popping crease measuring 8ft 8in (2.64m) wide by 4ft (1.22m) deep.

Beyond the boundary fence, directly behind each wicket is a moveable white sight screen. This is positioned so the batsman can clearly see the movement of the bowler's arm against the light background.

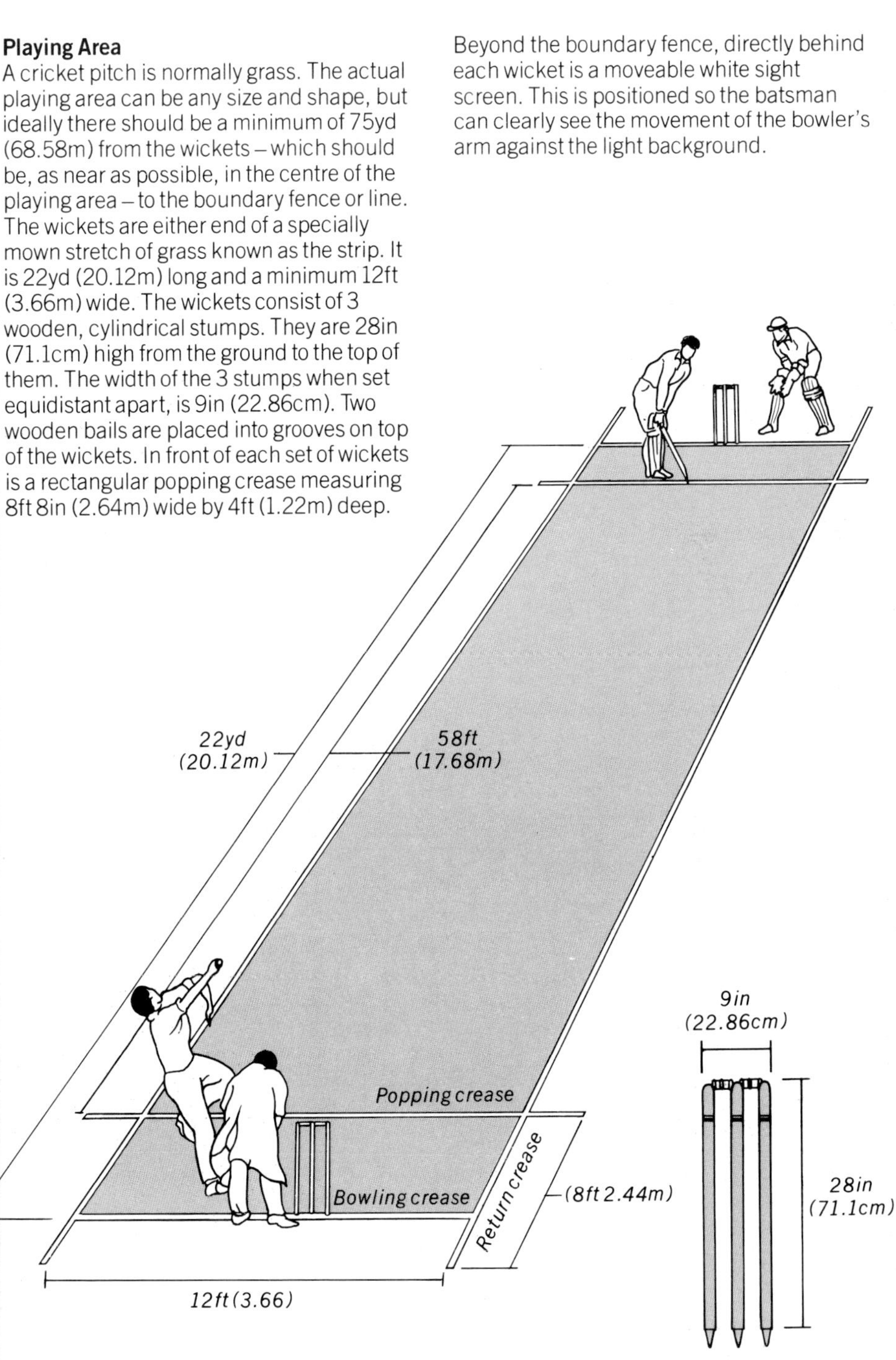

Starting Play
The 2 captains toss a coin to decide which team bats first. The team that does not bat becomes the bowling side and all their players take up their field positions. Two batsmen from the other team take up positions and play commences with a bowler delivering the ball from one end of the pitch to the batsman at the other. A bowler delivers 6 balls in an over, at the end of which a different bowler bowls from the opposite end of the pitch. The receiving batsman attempts to hit the ball and run between the 2 sets of wickets if he so desires. If he does run, the batsman at the other end of the pitch must run also. If a delivery from the bowler is not retrieved by a fielder, and is not hit by the batsman, runs may still be scored. These are known as byes, or extras, and although credited to the team score, they are not credited to the batsman. When a batsman is out he is replaced by another batsman from his own team. When ten batsmen are dismissed the team's innings is ended and they then become the fielding team and attempt to dismiss their opponents. In one-day cricket, once a team has surpassed the opponents score in the allocated number of overs the game is ended. In 3 and 5 day cricket, once a team has surpassed the combined total of runs of their opponent's 2 innings, the game is over.

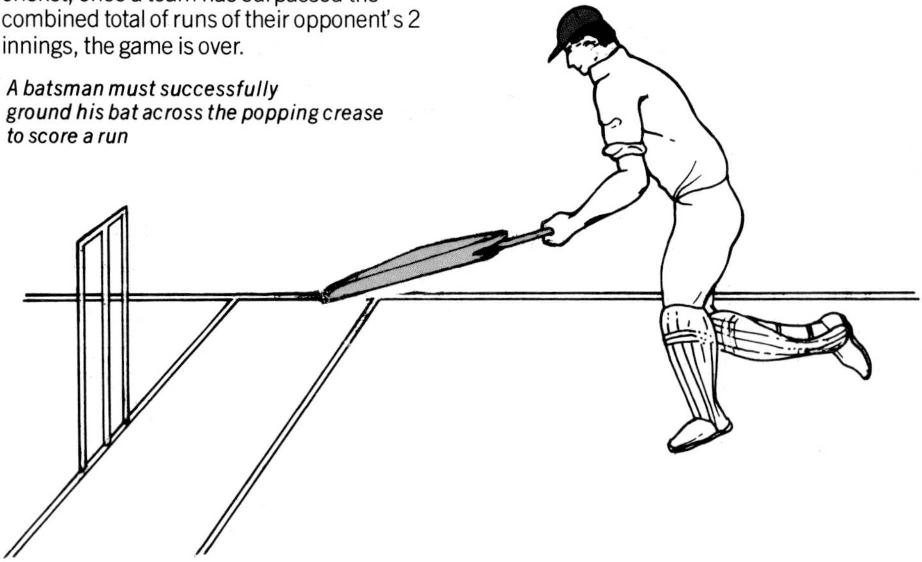

A batsman must successfully ground his bat across the popping crease to score a run

Scoring Runs
Runs are scored, as their name implies, by the batsmen running from one wicket to the next. For the run to be legal he must successfully ground his bat across the popping crease at the end to where he runs. Batsmen can run as many times as they like in between the wickets but runs of more than 3 are rare. Any ball reaching the perimeter is automatically worth 4 runs without the batsmen having to run. If the ball crosses the boundary without first hitting the ground it is 6 runs.

Declaring and the Follow On
In 3 and 5 day cricket, a team may declare an innings closed in an effort to get a result rather than let the game end as a draw. A team may declare at any time, and may even forfeit an innings. But the fact that they declare with say, 5 wickets remaining, does not affect the outcome of the match; it is their score that counts rather than wickets lost.

In 2 innings matches the side which bats first and leads by 200 in a 5 day match, or by 150 in a 3 day match shall have the option of asking the opposing side to bat again in successive innings.

Forms of Dismissal

BOWLED
The batsman is out bowled if the ball hits the wicket following a delivery from the bowler, even if the ball first touches his bat or person. At least one of the bails must be dislodged from the wicket for a batsman to be bowled out.

CAUGHT
A batsman is out if a fielder catches the ball before it hits the ground, after it has struck his bat, hand or glove below the wrist that is holding the bat.

HANDLED THE BALL
A batsman is out handled-ball if he touches the ball, with the hand not holding the bat, without the consent of the opposing side.

HIT THE BALL TWICE
If, after stopping the ball with his bat or his person, a batsman strikes the ball again, except to guard his wicket, he shall be dismissed for hitting the ball twice.

TIMED OUT
A new batsman shall be timed-out if he wilfully takes more than 2 minutes from the last dismissal to the time he steps on to the field of play.

HIT WICKET
If the batsman removes a bail either in preparing for a delivery, while receiving a delivery, or setting off on a run, with his bat or any part of his person or clothing, he is out hit wicket.

LEG BEFORE WICKET
If the batsman attempts to hit the ball and it strikes any part of his person before hitting the bat, and the ball would have hit the wicket, he is out leg before wicket (lbw). The ball must have pitched in a straight line between wicket and wicket or on the offside of the striker's wicket. Or in the case of a full toss, been judged certain to have pitched in that straight line.
A batsman is also out lbw if he makes no attempt to strike the ball if, in the opinion of the umpire, the ball would have hit the wicket as in the conditions already mentioned.

OBSTRUCTING THE FIELD
Either the receiving, or non-receiving batsman can be out for obstructing the field if he wilfully does so by words or action.

Bowled

LBW

Caught behind

RUN OUT
If a batsman fails to ground his bat or some part of his person in the popping crease before a fielder hits the wicket with the ball, the batsman is run out. If the 2 batsmen have crossed during their run then the one running towards the wicket hit is out. If they have not crossed, the one who left the wicket is the dismissed batsman.

STUMPED
If after making a stroke the batsman is out of his ground (the popping crease) and the wicket keeper puts down his wicket before any other fielder has touched the ball, then he has been stumped.

When a dismissal is not obvious, the fielding side must appeal to the umpire, by asking: "How's That?" before a batsman can be given out..

Stumped

The Bowler

The bowler is credited in the scorebook for the following dismissals: bowled, caught, lbw, stumped. If a bowler delivers a no-ball the batsman cannot be out except for the following: (a) run out (b) for obstructing the field (c) for hitting the ball twice. There are many ways a bowler can be called for no-balling but the most common are for (a) if more than 2 fielders are behind square of the batsman on the leg side as the ball is delivered (b) if, at the moment of delivery, the bowler has at least some part of his front foot behind the popping crease, and both feet within, and not touching, the return crease. (c) throwing the ball. If a bowler delivers a no-ball, or a ball that is wide, one run, plus any the batsmen may run, are added to the batting side's score but are not included in the bowler's statistics. The same applies to byes.

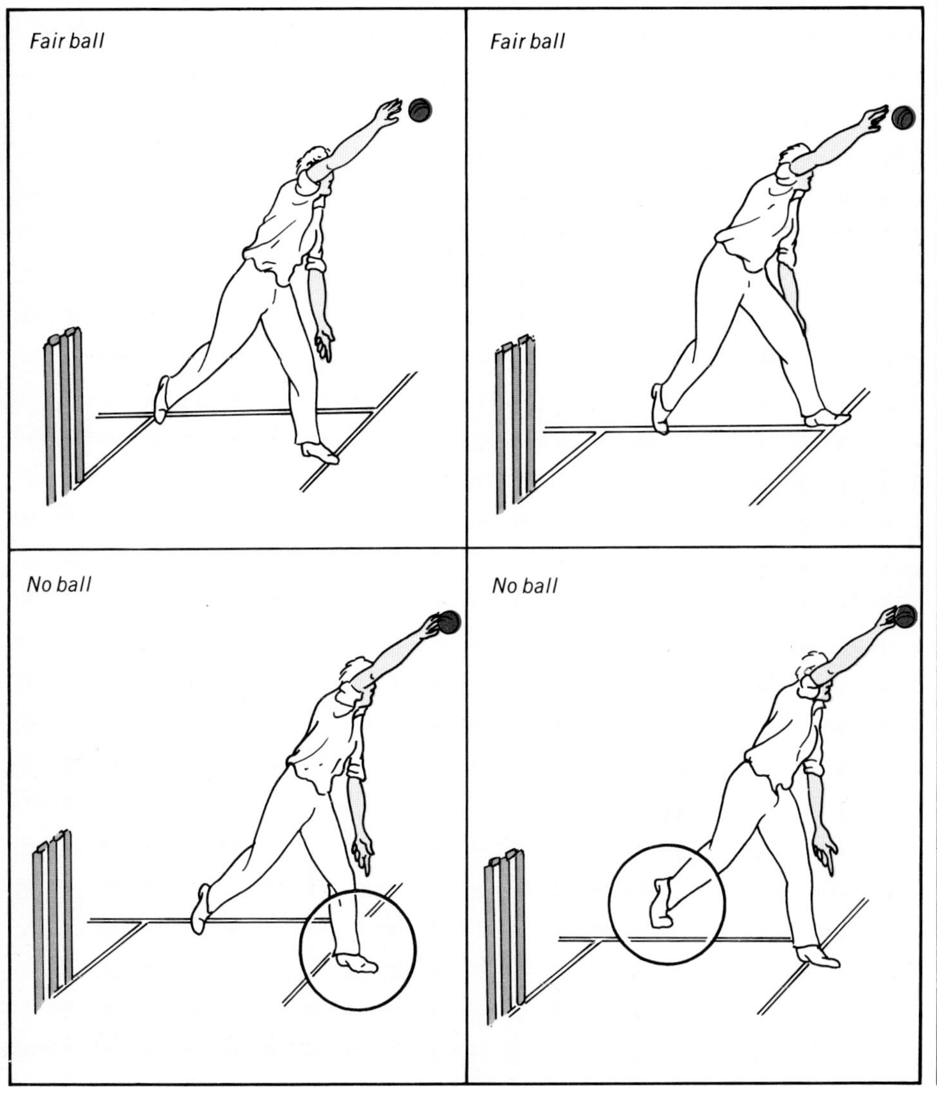

DUNCAN FEARNLEY
test
V
12

Clothing
All white clothing is a requisite (except for floodlit cricket when coloured clothing is essential). White pullovers with club or county colours are also worn in the colder weather. Batsmen wear protective gloves, leg pads, body pads and plastic groin boxes under their clothing. Steel helmets with a face mask, resembling an American Footballer, are now popular among professional cricketers. The wicketkeeper also wears pads to the legs and has large, well padded gloves. Some fielders, who stand close to the wicket, occasionally wear protective headgear.

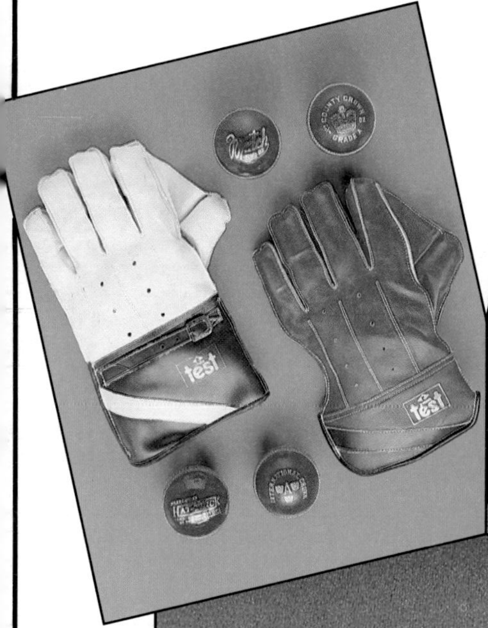

Cricketers wear white or cream shirts and flanneled trousers. The leather or canvas boots have spiked or barred soles for grip. Wicketkeepers wear heavy gauntlet-style gloves for protection and batsmen also wear strong gloves with the backs of the fingers protected by rubber or padding.

Cricket balls are made of a cork and twine core with a red leather outer casing and a stitched seam.

The early cricket bats were shaped like hockey sticks. Since the 19th century they have been straight-sided with a bulge – the "meat" – at the back running to the bottom or "toe". The blade is carved from willow and the handle made of cane, re-inforced with layers of rubber and bound in twine. The rubber grip over the handle extends into the bat in a V-shape which is known as the splice. The modern trend is towards lighter bats, between 2lb 4oz (1029gms) to 2lb 6oz (1077gms).

PATRICK
David Gower
All Ground
test
trent
NIKE
PATRICK
David Gower
Technique

Darts

Darts is one of the most popular of all games and can be played by any number of players, although 2 or 4 are the most common.

Darts can be traced back to Roman and Greek times when they used weighted throwing arrows in warfare. As a pastime, it is believed the Pilgrim Fathers played a form of darts while on board the *Mayflower* as they made their way to the New World in 1620. It has been known as a sport in its present form since 1896 when Lancastrian Brian Gamlin devised the present numbering system of the dart board. The National Darts Association was formed in 1924.

Object

To reach a pre-agreed score quicker than your opponent. The winner is the person who gets their score down to nil first, providing the last score is achieved by means of scoring a *double*.

Duration
A darts match does not last for a fixed period of time. The duration is decided by the score which each player is required to obtain. It is generally 501, but is often 101, 301, 701 or even 1001. A match constitutes a certain number of games (called legs) and can be over any pre-determined number of legs which build into sets.

Many modern day tournaments have an agreed number of games in a set (but it must be an odd number), and a certain amount of sets (again an odd number) constitute the match – similar to tennis.

For a game of 301 or less the players are normally required to start the game with a double, as well as finishing on a double.

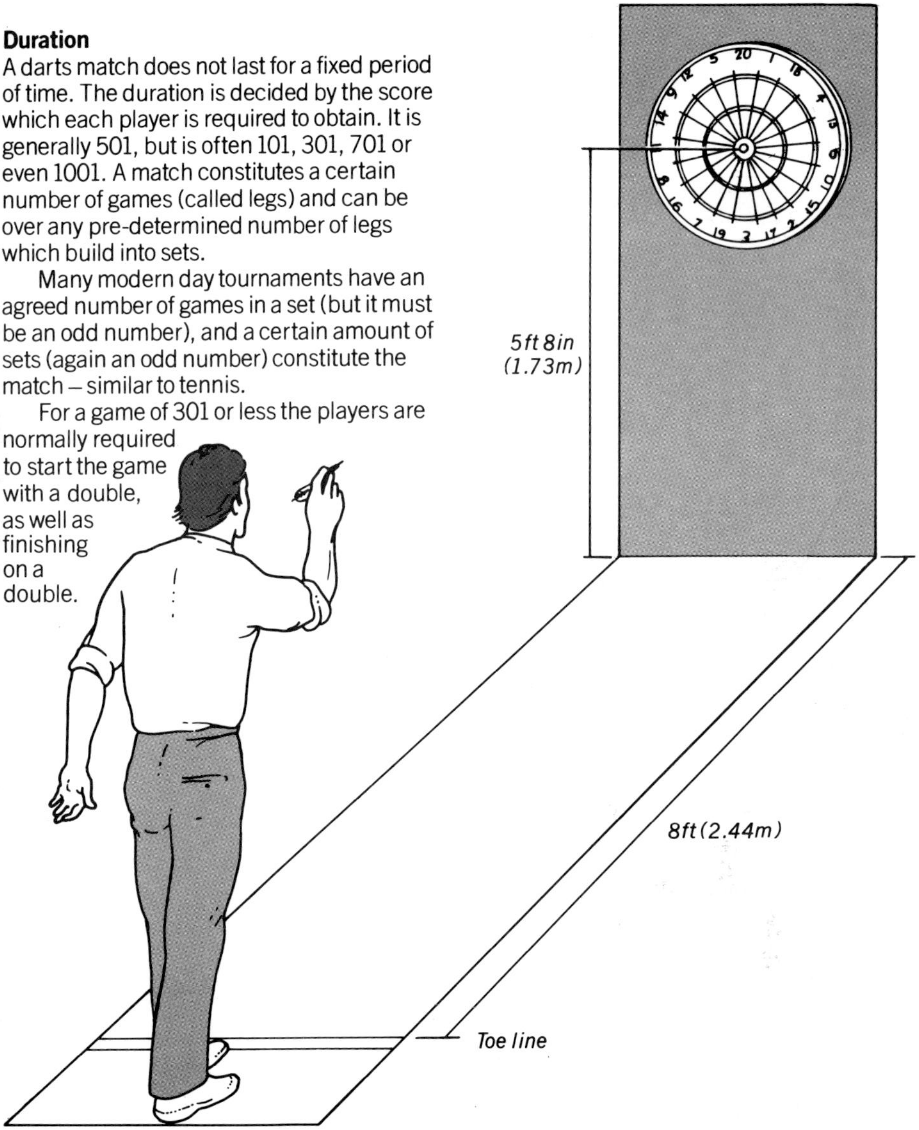

5ft 8in (1.73m)

8ft (2.44m)

Toe line

Players
The most popular game is singles with one player opposing another. However, doubles are regularly played with each player taking it in turn to throw.

Officials
A game is controlled by a referee who calls out a player's score after the completion of his throw. He also tells the player the score required if it is possible for him to complete the game in 3 darts. The referee is assisted by a scorer who marks each player's score after every 3 darts, and also indicates his reduced total.

Equipment
As the object is to throw arrows at a board and score as many points as possible, the board and arrows (darts) are the 2 requisites

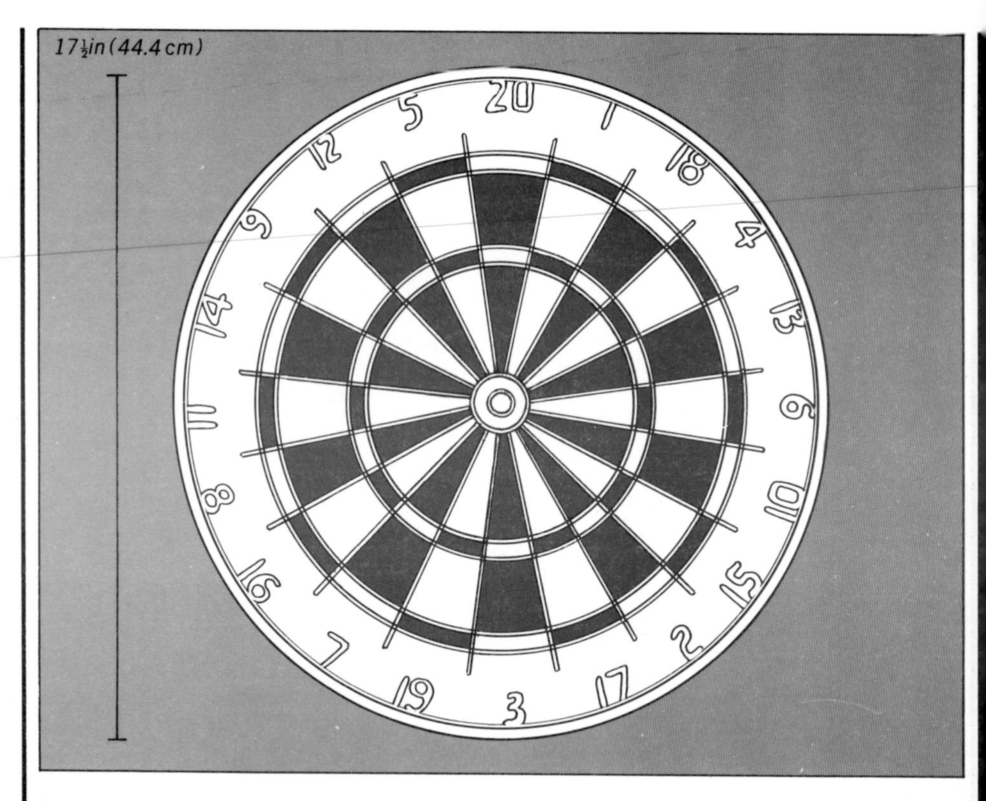

for a game.

The board is circular and divided by a thin wire into 20 equal segments numbered 1-20 but not in numerical order. There is an outer ring around the outside of the scoring area known as the double ring. Each number has a double ring and a dart entering that section scores double the appropriate number. Another ring, known as the inner ring, can be found between the outer ring and the centre of the board. This is known as the treble ring and if a dart enters that, then three times the appropriate score is obtained. The highest possible number to score with one dart is therefore treble 20, i.e. 60.

Two more smaller rings can be found at the centre of the board. The smaller one is called the *bullseye* and is worth 50 points, while the one surrounding it, often known as the *semi-bull* is worth 25 points.

The board should be positioned flat against a wall, and the height from the floor to the centre of the *bull* must be 5ft 8in (1.73m).

The diameter of the board is approximately 17½in (44.4cm).

A player must stand with his feet 8ft (2.44m) from the board although this distance can vary according to local rules and is often nearer for female players.

Dart boards are made in a variety of materials: cork, bristle, wood or plasticine and compressed paper. The bristle boards are the most popular.

The darts are made to various specifications to suit each individual player's needs. The weight is the all-important factor. The most popular weight range is ½-1oz (18-28g). It is imperative that the flight is undamaged otherwise the dart will not fly truly through the air. Modern day flights are made of plastic whereas they used to be made of feathers, or even cardboard. Feathered flights are still popular with some older players.

Up to a few years ago the dart came in two parts, the barrel and the shaft, complete with flight. Now, the barrel, normally made of tungsten, comes separate from the shaft, and the flights also come separate, thus enabling the player to select all three sections to suit his personal preference.

Starting Play
A toss of coin decides which player goes first. If a match consists of more than one game, the 1st throw alternates after each game.

In a game of 501 the players go straight off, and start scoring immediately without a double. The total obtained with 3 darts is noted and deducted from 501. The second player has his 3 throws and so on until either player gets down to a score requiring one of the doubles available on the board (the bull counts as double 25). Once a player has reached his score by completing the game on a double, the game is over, irrespective of who played first.

If a player exceeds his required score he reverts back to his old score.

In games that require a double to start, the player does not start scoring until he obtains a double. That score, plus other subsequent scores, then count.

Finishes
Most professionals like to leave double 16 as a finish because if they miss and hit a single 16 is is adjacent to double 8 which will be their next shot. The highest possible finish is 170 – treble 20, treble 20, bullseye (double 25). The next is 167 – treble 20, treble 19, bullseye.

Other games
The dart board lends itself to a variety of other games, other than conventional darts, including football, cricket, 'killer', round the clock, Shanghai and fives.

Golf

Golf is a stick and ball game played by 1,2,3 or 4 people, either individually, or as teams. Golf was first mentioned in a Scottish Act of Parliament in 1457 when the game was discouraged because of the need for archery practice. The first set of rules were drawn up in 1744 following the formation of the Gentlemen Golfers of Edinburgh (later the Honourable Company of Edinburgh Golfers). The Royal and Ancient was founded 10 years later, but it was not for another 100 years, in 1860, that the first British Open was staged.

Object

To hit the ball from tee to hole in the least number of strokes and either complete a round or rounds in fewer strokes than your opponent(s) or win more holes than him.

Duration
There is no time limit for a round of golf. It ends when, in stroke play all 18 holes have been completed, or in the case of match-play when 1 player reaches a point where he cannot be beaten. In tournament play, the competition normally consists of 4 rounds held over 4 days.

Players
Two players can play against each other. Alternatively 3 players can play in what is known as a 'three-ball'. They can count their individual scores if stroke play, or, if match play, the single player can play against the best score of either of the other 2. If 4 players are together for a round they can count their individual scores or 2 can play against the other 2 as teams.

Officials
The referee is in sole charge of a golf match. His main duty is to resolve matters regarding points of law. In major events, marshalls are used to ensure crowds are controlled and that golfers have adequate room to play their shots. Markers indicate where each player's ball has come to rest.

Ball
The golf ball is round and has elastic thread wound around a central rubber core. The outside is covered in a plastic coating, normally white, which is indented with dimples to add greater velocity. The diameter of the ball should be not less than 1.62in (41.15mm). The larger American ball (now more commonly used) has a minimum diameter of 1.68in (42.67mm). The weight must not be greater than 1.62oz (45.93g).

Other Equipment
When playing the 1st shot from the teeing ground, the player is allowed to assist his drive by placing his ball

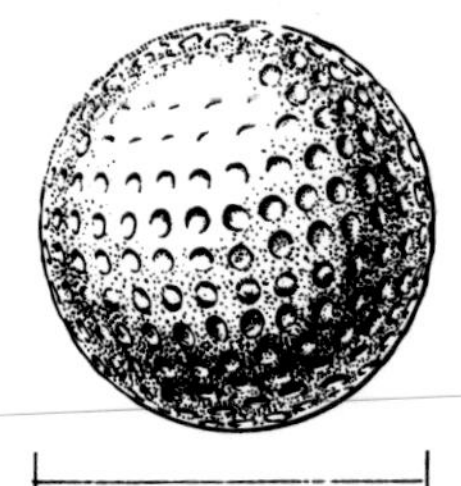

1.62in (41.15mm) or 1.68in (42.67mm)

on a small plastic, or wooden, tee. This raises the ball off the ground and increases the chance of a clean hit.

A player can pick up his ball (unless local rules state otherwise) only on the green. When he does so he can mark it with a small plastic disc.

Clubs
A golfer is not allowed to carry more than 14 clubs in his bag. Most take a putter, four woods of different loft for driving and playing long fairway shots, and nine irons ranging from a No.1 iron to a sand wedge, all of which have different angled faces, and serve specific purposes.

A Driver 12
B 2 wood 14
C 4 wood 20
2 Iron 19
3 Iron 23
4 Iron 27
5 Iron 31
6 Iron 35
7 Iron 39
8 Iron 43
9 Iron 47
P.W. Pitching wedge
S.W. Sand wedge

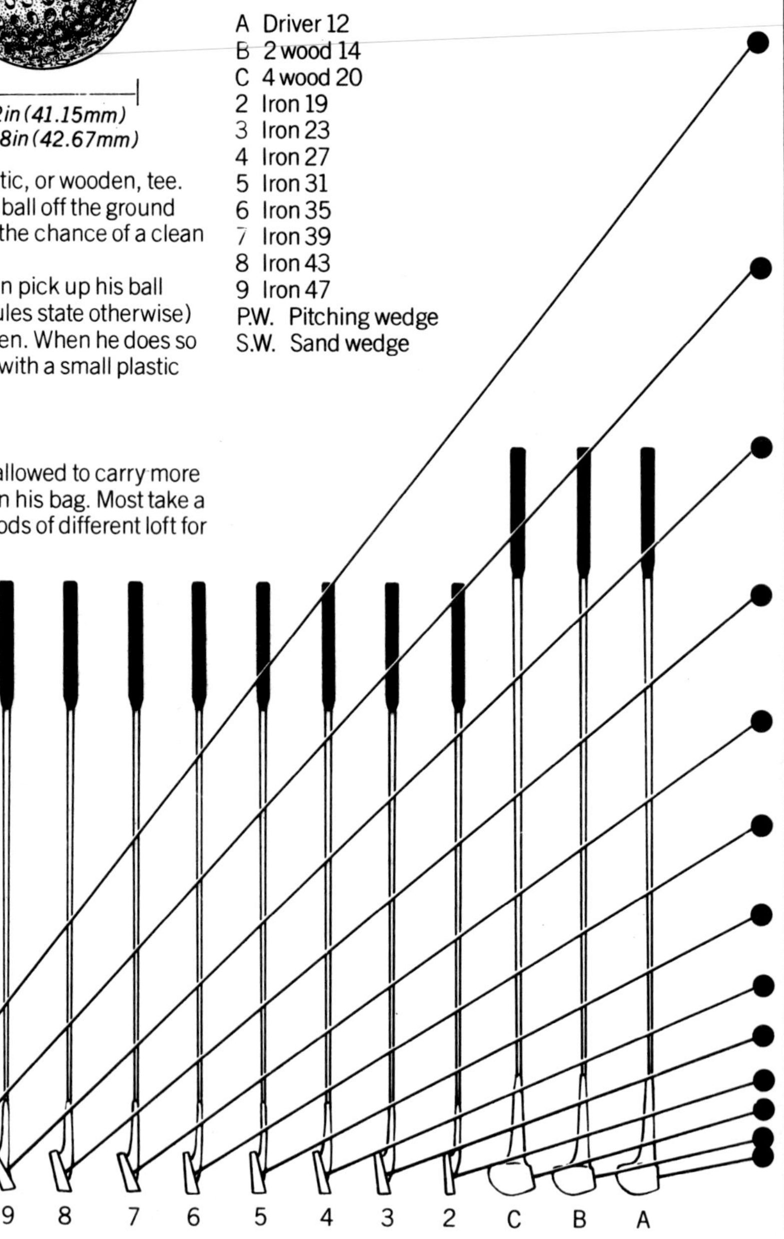

Playing Area
There are no regulations regarding the size of the actual area taken by a golf course, and indeed no regulations for the length of each hole. Most courses are 18 holes long, although many 9 hole, and some 15 hole courses exist. The design of each individual hole depends on the terrain of the course. The par of the course is based on the length of each hole which can vary from 100-600 yd (91.44-548.64m) approximately.

Each hole consists of a teeing area, the fairway, and green. In the green is set a hole into which the player is ultimately attempting to get the ball. A flagstick indicates the position of the hole on each green.

Each green is numbered 1-18 (or 1-9) and must be played in correct sequence. Hazards, like streams, trees, sand-filled bunkers, are often found in the area between the teeing area and the green to make play that more testing.

Starting a Game

The players decide by a toss of a coin which one tees off first. After all players have played from the teeing area the person furthest away from the hole plays next, and so on. The hole is completed when both, or all, players have put their ball in the hole, or in the case of match-play, the hole conceded. The player winning the hole goes first at the next tee and he retains that honour until he loses a hole.

Match-Play/Stroke-Play

A round of stroke-play golf consists of playing every hole and recording each player's score at each of the 18 holes. The player with the lowest score is the winner.

In match-play, the idea is to win more holes than your opponent by taking fewer shots at each hole. If 2 players have the same score at a hole then that is called a half and nobody wins that hole. Once a player reaches a position where his opponent cannot overtake him, the game ends. For example, if a person has won 3 more holes than his opponent and only 2 holes remain, the round ends and that player is said to have won 3 and 2.

Fourball/Foursomes

Both are matches involving 4 players. The former is played by one pair against another with the better score of the 2 players being recorded at each hole. Alternatively the aggregate score at the end of the round can count. In a foursomes match, 2 play against 2, but each team must play alternate strokes at the same ball. However, irrespective of who played the last shot at the previous hole, they must take alternate turns at driving. Both forms of play are suited to match-play and stroke-play conditions.

Handicapping

Golf is one of those games where the great can play alongside the most mediocre of players thanks to a handicap system which sets out to make all players equal.

Handicaps are graded from scratch (0) up to 30 and, in the case of a stroke-play round, the handicap is deducted from the gross score to give a net score. In match-play conditions the player with the higher handicap receives $\frac{3}{4}$ the difference between the 2 handicaps and, say that figure is 6, he is allowed a stroke at the 6 most difficult holes on the course as indicated by the stroke on the score-card.

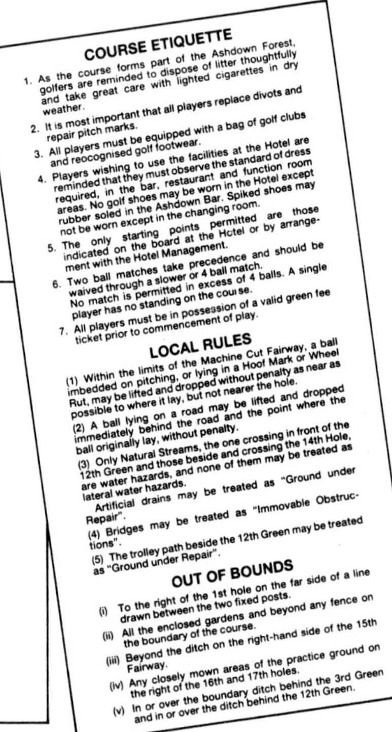
COURSE ETIQUETTE

1. As the course forms part of the Ashdown Forest, golfers are reminded to dispose of litter thoughtfully and take great care with lighted cigarettes in dry weather.
2. It is most important that all players replace divots and repair pitch marks.
3. All players must be equipped with a bag of golf clubs and reocognised golf footwear.
4. Players wishing to use the facilities at the Hotel are reminded that they must observe the standard of dress required, in the bar, restaurant and function room areas. No golf shoes may be worn in the Hotel except rubber soled in the Ashdown Bar. Spiked shoes may not be worn except in the changing room.
5. The only starting points permitted are those indicated on the board at the Hotel or by arrangement with the Hotel Management.
6. Two ball matches take precedence and should be waived through a slower or 4 ball match. No match is permitted in excess of 4 balls. A single player has no standing on the course.
7. All players must be in possession of a valid green fee ticket prior to commencement of play.

LOCAL RULES

(1) Within the limits of the Machine Cut Fairway, a ball imbedded on pitching, or lying in a Hoof Mark or Wheel Rut, may be lifted and dropped without penalty as near as possible to where it lay, but not nearer the hole.

(2) A ball lying on a road may be lifted and dropped immediately behind the road and the point where the ball originally lay, without penalty.

(3) Only Natural Streams, the one crossing in front of the 12th Green and those beside and crossing the 14th Hole, are water hazards, and none of them may be treated as lateral water hazards.

Artificial drains may be treated as "Ground under Repair".

(4) Bridges may be treated as "Immovable Obstructions".

(5) The trolley path beside the 12th Green may be treated as "Ground under Repair".

OUT OF BOUNDS

(i) To the right of the 1st hole on the far side of a line drawn between the two fixed posts.

(ii) All the enclosed gardens and beyond any fence on the boundary of the course.

(iii) Beyond the ditch on the right-hand side of the 15th Fairway.

(iv) Any closely mown areas of the practice ground on the right of the 16th and 17th holes.

(v) In or over the boundary ditch behind the 3rd Green and in or over the ditch behind the 12th Green.

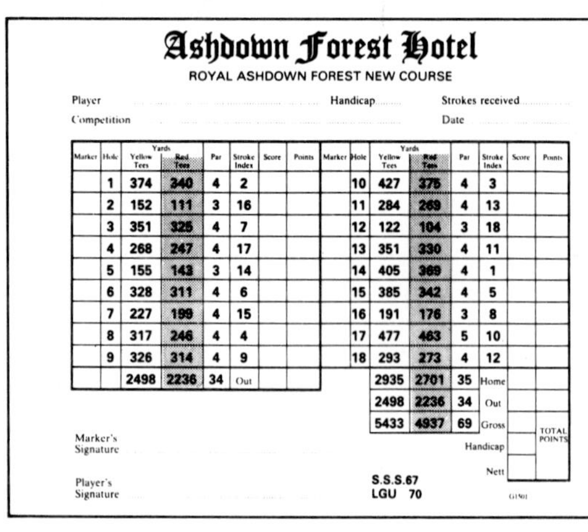
Ashdown Forest Hotel

ROYAL ASHDOWN FOREST NEW COURSE

Player .... Handicap .... Strokes received ....

Competition .... Date ....

Marker	Hole	Yards Yellow Tees	Yards Red Tees	Par	Stroke Index	Score	Points	Marker	Hole	Yards Yellow Tees	Yards Red Tees	Par	Stroke Index	Score	Points
	1	374	340	4	2				10	427	375	4	3		
	2	152	111	3	16				11	284	269	4	13		
	3	351	325	4	7				12	122	104	3	18		
	4	268	247	4	17				13	351	330	4	11		
	5	155	143	3	14				14	405	369	4	1		
	6	328	311	4	6				15	385	342	4	5		
	7	227	199	4	15				16	191	176	3	8		
	8	317	246	4	4				17	477	463	5	10		
	9	326	314	4	9				18	293	273	4	12		
		2498	2236	34	Out					2935	2701	35	Home		
										2498	2236	34	Out		
										5433	4937	69	Gross		TOTAL POINTS
													Handicap		
													Nett		

Marker's Signature

Player's Signature

S.S.S.67

LGU 70

G1501

Terminology
Golf uses a terminology unique to the sport.

PAR the number of strokes one is expected to take for a specific hole and for the complete round.

BIRDIE a hole completed in one stroke under par.

EAGLE a hole completed in 2 strokes under par.

ALBATROSS a hole completed in 3 strokes under par (and, like the albatross, a very rare bird).

BOGEY a hole competed in one over par.

DOUBLE BOGEY a hole completed in 2 over par.

Penalties
Penalty strokes can be incurred for a variety of infringement of rules. The most common causes of penalty are for a lost ball, a ball being unplayable, and a ball going out of bounds.

Clothing
The modern day golfer is equipped with leather, or rubberized, shoes fitted with spikes for a good grip. He also wears a glove on his left hand (if right-handed) to improve grip, and carries, in his bag, water-proof jacket and trousers ready for the bad weather, and a large colourful umbrella. The better quality bags are made of leather and are sometimes transported by a trolley.

Etiquette
Most of golf etiquette is common sense and good manners:

A player must not stand in the range of an opponent who is making a stroke, or talk to him.

He should replace divots on the fairway and repair any damage done to the green by his ball or shoes.

No player should play a shot until all players in front are out of range.

After leaving a bunker a player should level out the sand and fill all marks left by him.

When looking for a lost ball, after a reasonable period of time, a player should call other players through.

Observe the rules of precedure: 2-ball matches have precedence over 3 and 4 -ball matches, and should be called through. A player on his own has no standing on the golf course.

Golf trolleys take the strain out of carrying a heavy bagful of clubs.

The rules of golf allow for a maximum of 14 clubs to be carried during a competitive round. Usually this comprises four woods, seven irons, a sand wedge, a pitching wedge and a putter.

The wooden clubs have longer shafts and are used to achieve distance. The striking faces of the irons are inclined at progressive angles from 19°. The higher the number of the club the higher its trajectory and, consequently, the shorter its distance. The sand wedge is used for bunker shots and the wedge for short approach shots or retrieving from heavy rough.

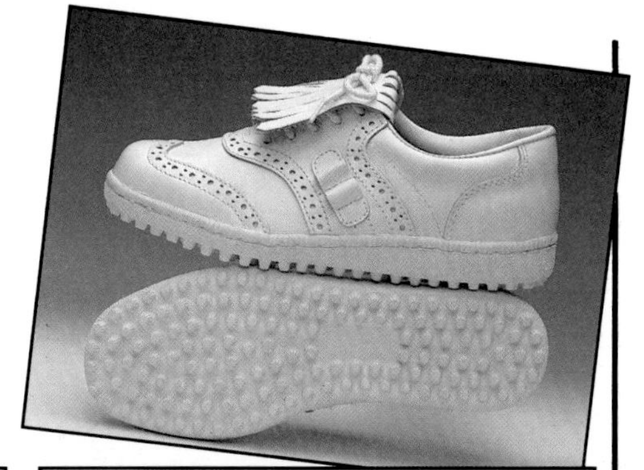

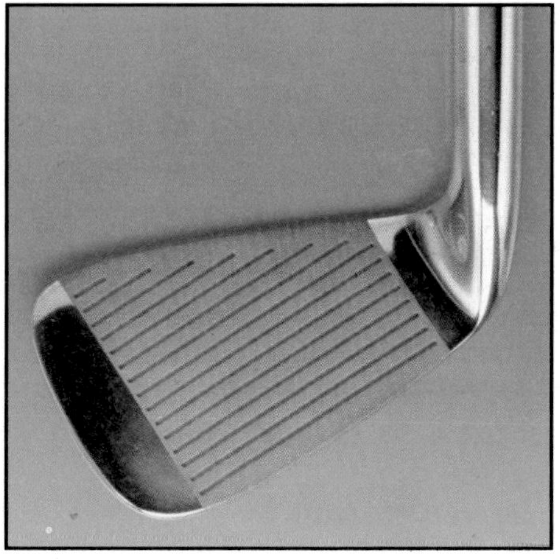

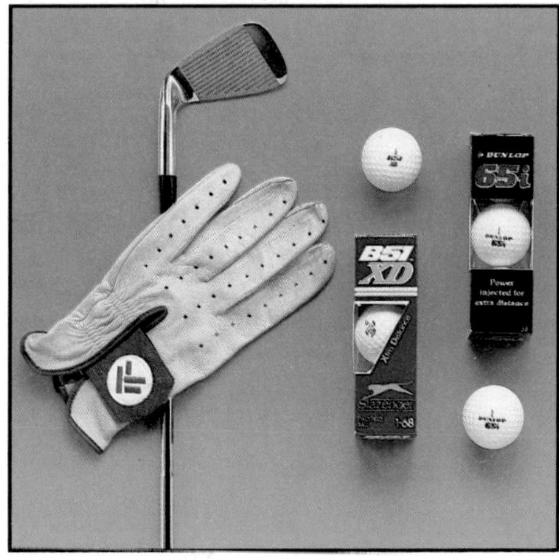

The golf ball is made of elastic thread wound under tension around a central core and covered in a plastic, dimpled casting.

Right handed golfers wear a glove on their left hand to aid grip.

Hockey

Hockey is a non-physical contact stick and ball game played by 2 teams of men or women with 11 players per side. The indoor variety of the game is played by 6 players per team.

The Greeks, Arabs and Romans all played a form of hockey. The naming of the sport is thought to have come in the 16th century when the Galway Statutes mentioned 'Hockie'. It became popular in the mid 19th century and the first club was Blackheath, formed in 1861.

Object
To propel the ball with the stick into your opponents' goal, and score more goals than the opposing team.

Duration
A game normally lasts 70 minutes, divided into 2 halves of 35 minutes each with an interval of 5 or 10 minutes in between. Teams change ends at the interval.

Teams
There are 11 players in each team and the formations used are similar to soccer (ie 1-4-2-4, 1-1-3-2-4, 1-1-3-3-3) although many sides are now reverting to the 1-2-3-5 system as their foundation.

Officials
Two umpires control the game, and it is essential their clothing in no way resembles that of either team. Each umpire operates from one half of the pitch for the entire game and on opposite side lines.

Ball
The ball weighs between 5½ and 5¾oz (156-163g) and has a circumference of between 8 and 9in (224-23.5cm). The ball may have a hollow or solid centre and may be made of any natural or artificial material provided that it is hard, with a smooth outer surface.

Stick
There are no rules governing the length of a stick but the average length is 3ft (91.44cm). The weight of a stick varies between 12-28oz (340.2-793.8g) for men and 12-23oz (340.2-652.05g) for women. The whole stick must be able to pass through a ring with a 2in (5.08cm) diameter. The head must be wooden and have a flat face. A player is allowed to use only one stick at a time and must play the ball with the face of it.

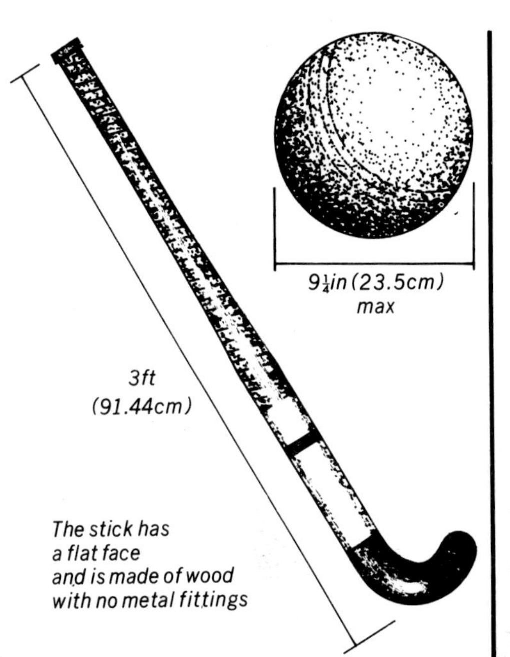

The stick has a flat face and is made of wood with no metal fittings

Each team has a goal keeper 2 backs, 3 halves and 5 forwards

Playing Area

The most common playing surface is grass although artificial surfaces are becoming more popular. The pitch is rectangular and is 100yd (91.44m) long and between 55-60yd (50-55m) wide. The longer boundary lines are called side lines and the shorter ones are goal lines. All lines markings are 3in (7.62cm) wide. A centre line is drawn across the middle of the pitch, dividing the 2 halves of the field, and a broken line is drawn 25yd (22m) from each goal line and parallel to it. At either end of the pitch is a goal 12ft (3.66m) wide and 7ft (2.13m) high, to which is attached a net with a stop board inside it. In front of each goal is a semi-circle known as the striking or shooting circle.

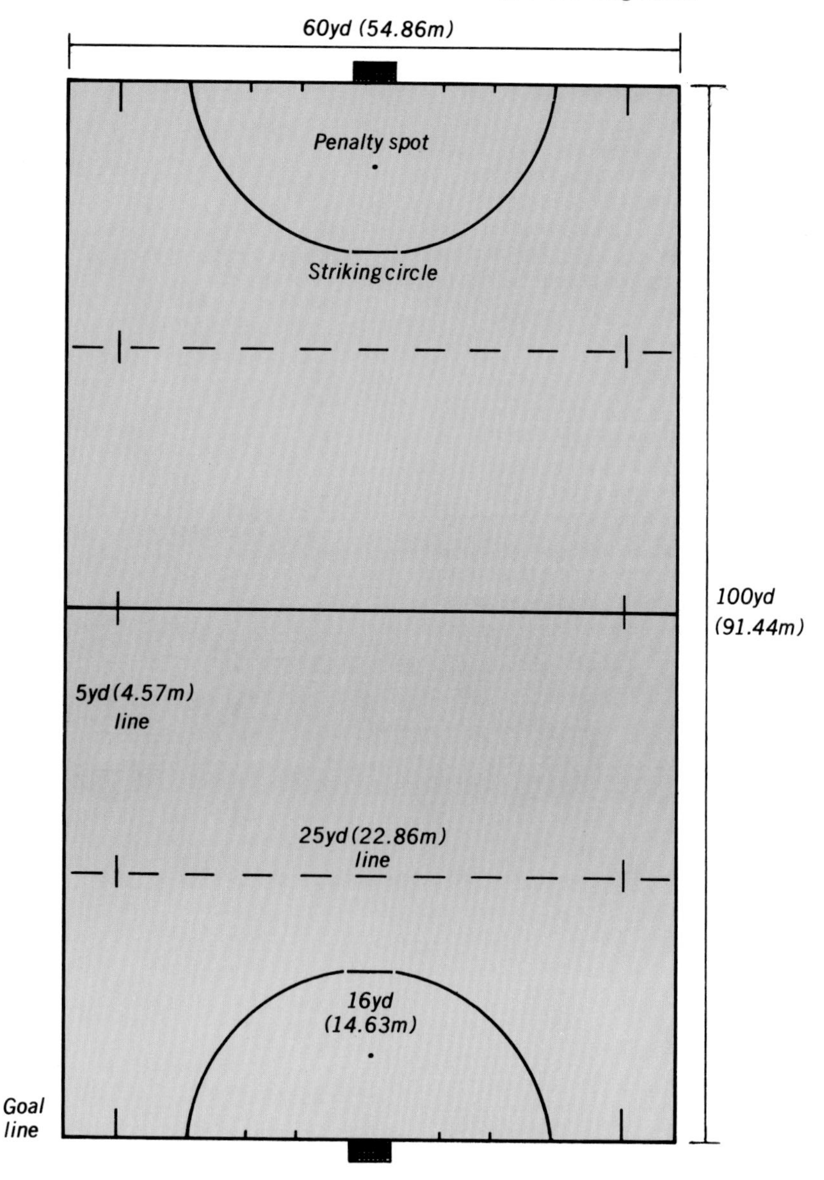

Starting Play

The game is started and restarted after a goal by a pass-back at the centre of the field. At the moment of the pass-back players must be in their defending half of the field and none of the opposing team may be within 5yd (4.57m) of the ball. The pass may be a hit or push but it must not be directed over the centre line. At the start of the game the captain winning the toss chooses to defend a particular end of the field or to take the pass-back.

Tactics and Scoring

The object is to get the ball into the opposing shooting circle and then score a goal. Goals can be scored *only* from inside the circle. For a goal to be valid, the entire ball must cross the goal line. Running with the ball (dribbling) and passing are the main attributes of a good hockey player. Proper control of the stick is also vital and it should be held firmly with both hands, and with the left above the right. When striking for goal the 2 hands should be close together. For other strokes the left hand grips the top of the stick while the right is moved to a comfortable position down the stick.

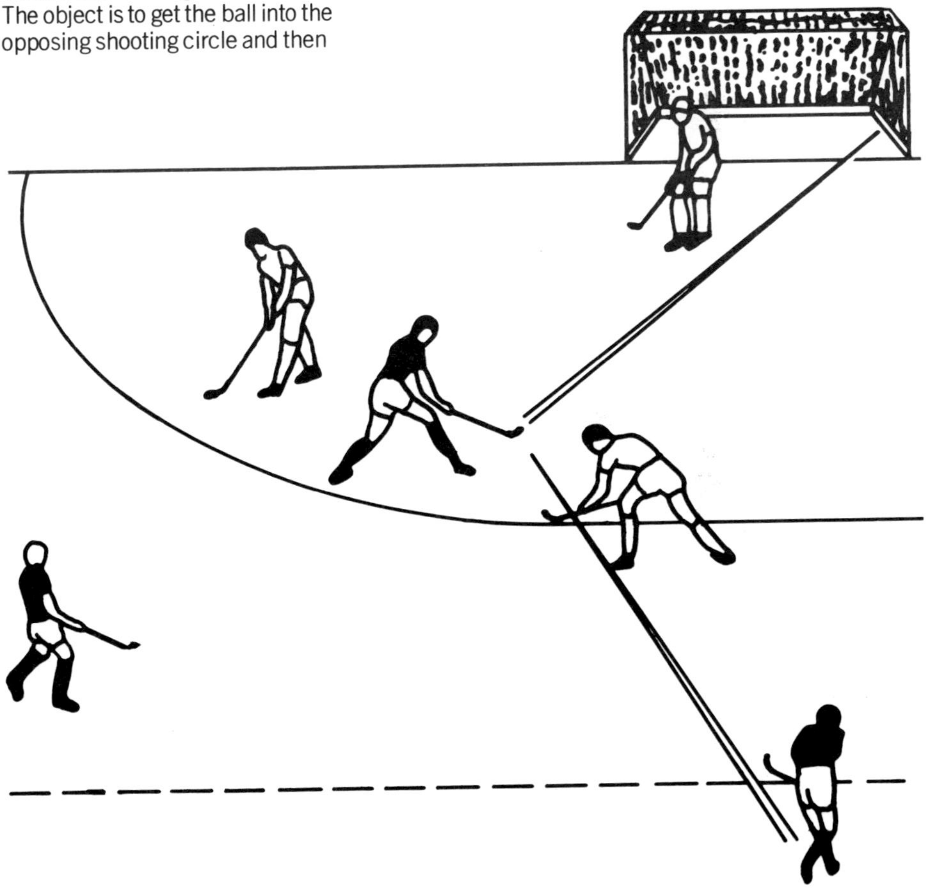

Fouls
A player is penalised if any part of the stick rises above his shoulders or he plays the ball in a dangerous manner. The penalty is a free hit from the spot where the offence occurred. Before the ball is struck, it must be motionless and no player of the opposing team is allowed within 5yd (4.57m) of it until another player has touched the ball. A player is not allowed to stop the ball with any part of his body, play the ball in a dangerous or potentially dangerous manner or make wild swings with the stick. Hitting, holding, or interfering with an opponent's stick also results in a penalty.

Push in

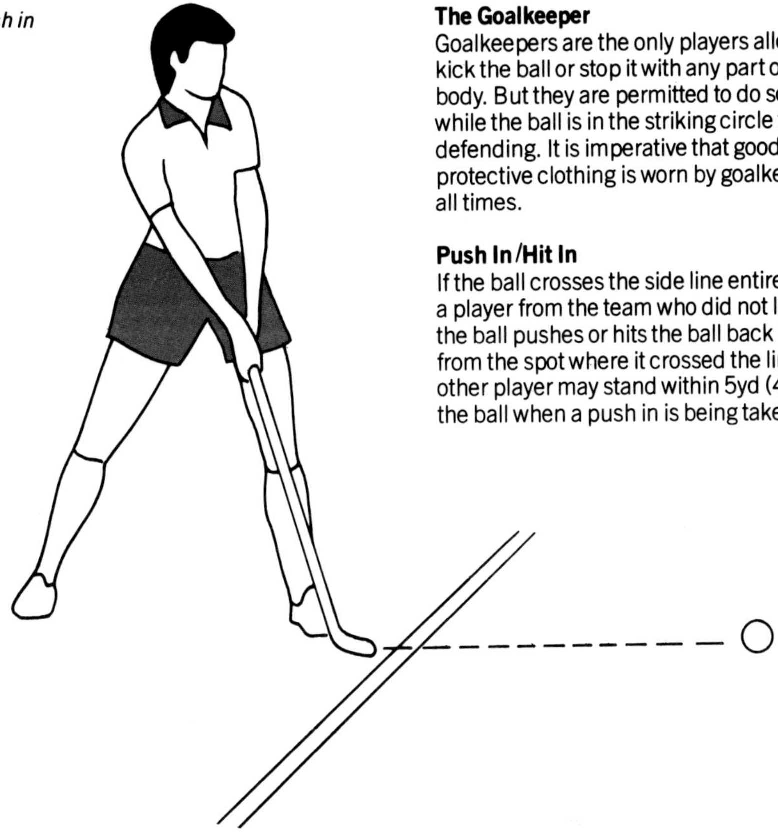

The Goalkeeper

Goalkeepers are the only players allowed to kick the ball or stop it with any part of their body. But they are permitted to do so only while the ball is in the striking circle they are defending. It is imperative that good quality protective clothing is worn by goalkeepers at all times.

Push In/Hit In

If the ball crosses the side line entirely, then a player from the team who did not last touch the ball pushes or hits the ball back into play from the spot where it crossed the line. No other player may stand within 5yd (4.57m) of the ball when a push in is being taken.

Corners

The method of starting play after the ball crosses the goal line when a goal has not been scored varies, depending upon whether the umpire decides that the ball was put out accidentally or intentionally.

If the attacking side put the ball over the line, or a defender puts it over unintentionally from outside his own 25yd (22.86m) area, play re-starts with a free hit to the defending side 16yd (14.63m) from the goal line, exactly opposite the spot where the ball crossed.

If a defender puts the ball out from inside his 25yd (22.86m) area the umpire will award a corner, but if the umpire feels he put the ball out deliberately he will award a penalty corner. In the first case a player of the attacking side pushes or hits the ball from a spot on the back line within 5yd (4.57m) of the corner flag. No other player of either side is allowed within 5yd (4.57m) of the ball when it is played.

At a penalty corner the attacking team must start outside the circle with the exception of the player injecting the ball, who does this from the back line at a point at least 10yd (9.14m) from the goal post on whichever side the attack prefers. The ball must be stopped before a shot is allowed unless it touches the stick of a defender. Only 6 defenders are allowed at a penalty corner and they must begin behind the back line and no closer than 5yd (4.57m) from the ball. The remainder of the defending team must be in the opposing half of the field. Penalty corners are also awarded for deliberate infringements inside their own 25yd (22.86m) area.

Penalty Stroke
For an intentional infringement by a defender in the shooting circle the umpire can award a penalty stroke. This is taken from a spot 7yd (6.4m) from the goal line, and between the posts. The goalkeeper must stand on his goal line, while his colleagues must stand outside the 25yd (22.86m) area. The attacking player is allowed to take only one pace forward before pushing or flicking the ball at goal.

Clothing
The 2 teams play in shirts, shorts and socks which must not clash with the colours of the opposing team. Footwear may be soccer boots, training shoes or special multi-studded boots depending on the type of pitch. Shinguards are essential and many players wear mouthguards to protect their teeth from a ball deflecting upwards off the stick.

Penalty stroke

Goalkeepers wear additional protective clothing including gloves, pads, kickers, chest pads, abdominal protectors and helmets, which are vital when facing balls travelling at nearly 100mph.

Ice Hockey

Ice hockey is the fastest team sport in the world. Teams consist of 6 players. Each has a stick and the object 'ball' is known as a puck.

Ice hockey can trace its origins to the 2nd century, but it is relatively new as a sport in its present form. The game was first played on ice, using a puck instead of a ball, by Englishmen at Kingston Harbour, Ontario, Canada, in 1860. Most of these pioneers were war veterans from the Crimea. Canada has remained the ice hockey centre of the world, and they claim the first organized club, the McGill University Hockey Club, Montreal, which was formed in 1880.

Object

To hit the puck into your opponent's goal more times than they hit it into yours.

Duration

A game is divided into 3 periods, each lasting 20 minutes. Only the periods when the puck is in play are timed. At all other moments the electronic watch is stopped. In between the 3 playing periods there are intervals of 10 minutes, during which time the ice is re-surfaced.

Teams

Six players are allowed on the ice at any one time, but because of the fast nature of the sport, substitutes are essential. Most teams consist of anything from 11 to 18 players. Substitutions can be made at any time during a game providing the puck is 'dead' and the substituted player has left the ice. The line up of the 6 players normally consists of a goalminder, 2 defenders and 3 forwards – a centreman and 2 wingers. It is not necessary to play a goalminder and some teams will sacrifice the goalminder in the closing minutes of a game in an effort to score a much needed goal.

Officials

A game is controlled by 2 referees, both on the ice simultaneously, who each control one half of the rink. They are assisted by goal judges at each end who indicate the score.

Playing line-up

1 goalminder

2 right defence

3 left defence

4 centre

5 right wing

6 left wing

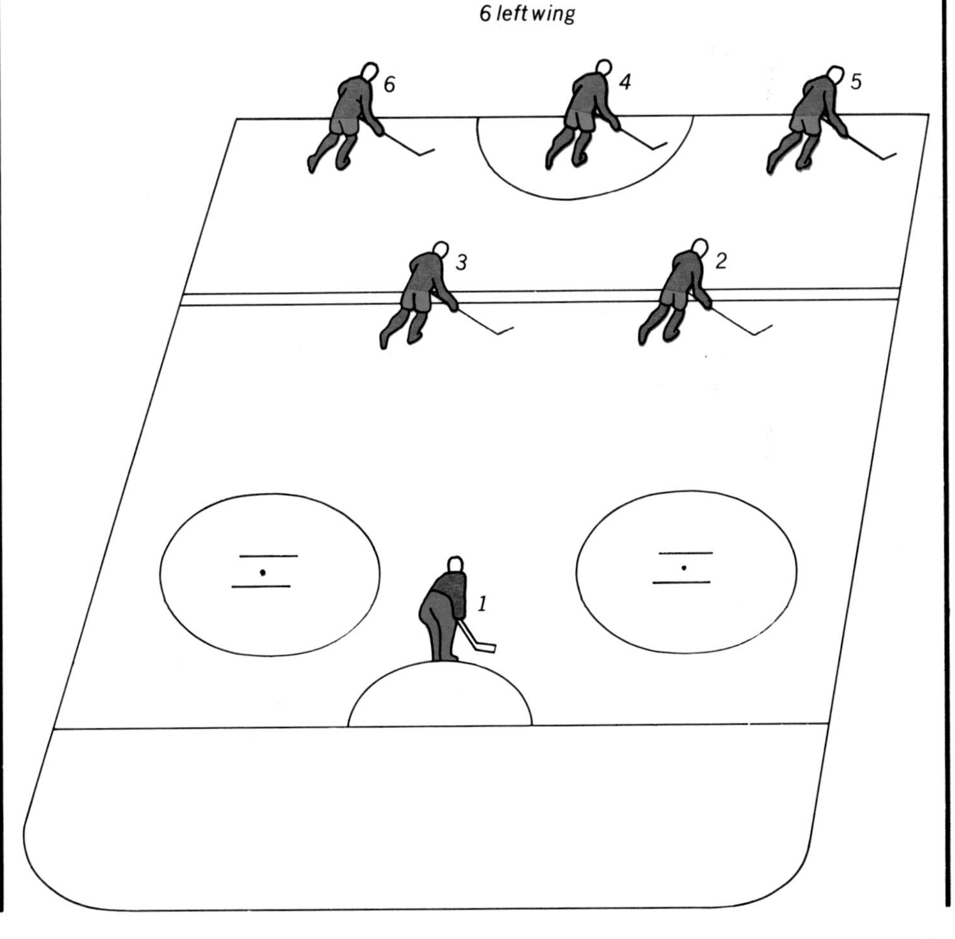

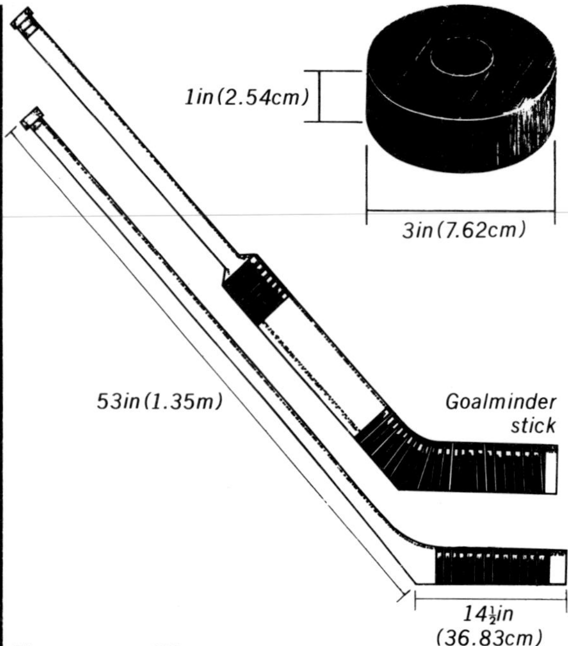

Puck
Disc-shaped, it is made of vulcanized rubber and is 3in (7.62cm) in diameter and 1in (2.54cm) thick. The puck weighs approximately 5½oz (155.93gm). Before play the puck is generally frozen so as to maintain its original form as long as possible.

Stick
Made entirely of laminated wood. The maximum length of the handle is 53in (1.35m) and the blade is limited to a maximum length of 14½in (36.83cm). The goalminder's stick, however, is wider and heavier. Sticks are chosen by a player's preference to the *lie* of the blade – in other words, the angle between the blade and handle. Generally, sticks are manufactured with 10 different lies.

There are ten different types of ice hockey stick, graded 1-10. The higher the number the more vertical the shaft. Their manufacture is a painstaking process with timber cut into strips and allowed to air dry for six months to ensure it is neither too rigid nor too springy. For the correct length, the top of the shaft should just touch the player's chin when the stick is held upright with the blade on the ice.

Boot and Skates
Ice hockey skates differ from figure and speed skates. The blade is thinner and shorter and does not have the toe-rake that can be found in figure skating. The boot has ankle supports, but is nowhere near as long as other forms of ice-skating boot. The blade is approximately 1/6in (0.42cm) wide.

Ice hockey skate

Ice hockey skate blades are shorter than speed skates.

Playing Area

Ice hockey is played on either mechanically frozen or natural ice, although the former is more common. The playing area, called a rink, should ideally be 200ft (60.96m) long and 85ft (25.91m) wide and surrounded by protective barrier boards. These boards, which should be curved at each corner, should not be more than 4ft (1.22m) high or lower than 40in (1.02m).

Red goal lines are marked 10ft (3.05m) in from each end of the rink. In the middle of them are the goals 6ft (1.83m) wide and 4ft (1.22m) high. In front of each goal is a semi-circular goal crease with a 6ft (1.83m) radius.

Two blue lines, each 1ft (30.48cm) wide, divide the rink into 3 equal parts known as defence, neutral and attacking zones. A centre red line, also 1ft (30.48cm) wide, divides the rink into 2 halves. Across the centre line is drawn the face-off circle with a 30ft (9.14m) diameter and a blue spot which marks the centre. Four more circles are marked on the ice, 2 in each half. In addition 2 red face-off spots are marked between the centre spot and each blue line. When play needs to be re-started after an infringement, or for any other reason, it starts from the nearest face-off point to where the incident happened.

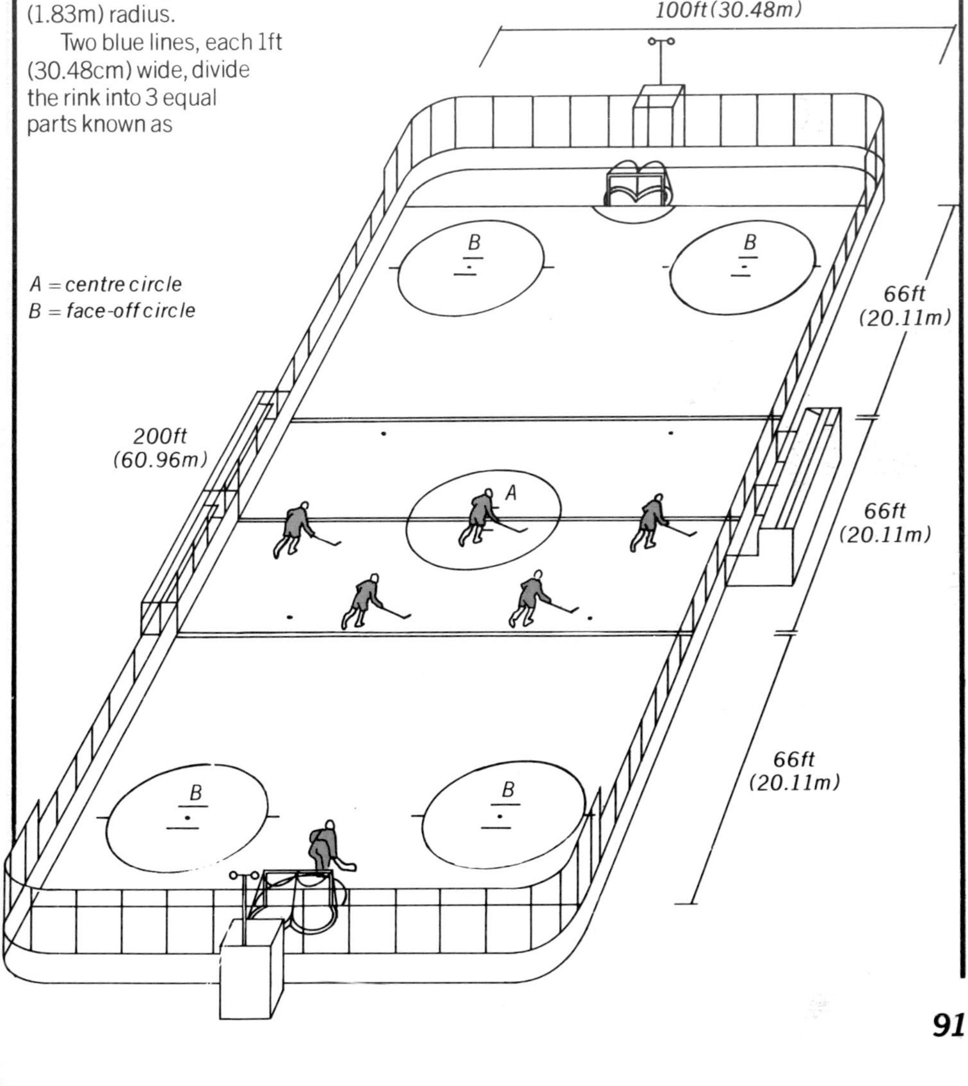

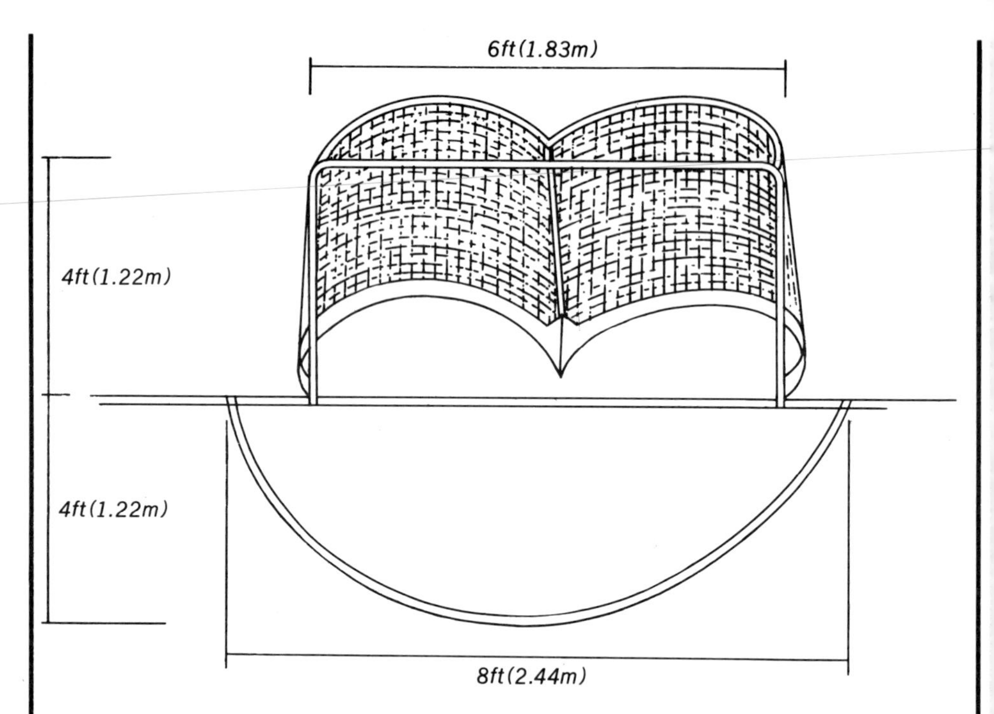

Starting Play

Play starts with a *face-off.* The two centremen face each other, at least one sticks length apart, and do battle as the referee drops the puck on the centre spot. No other player is allowed within 10ft (3.05m) of either centreman at the face-off. Each new period, and restart after the scoring of a goal, begins with a face-off in the centre circle. The puck remains in play until such time as it goes over the barrier board or the referee whistles for an infringement. Play is permitted behind the goals.

A goal is scored only if the puck is propelled into the goal with the stick. A goal is not allowed if the puck is kicked or thrown into the goal. If an attacking player is in the goal crease when a goal is scored it is disallowed.

A player is allowed to stop the puck with his hand or body and he is allowed to skate with the puck in his hand, but for no more than 3 seconds.

The face-off

Playing Zones
The playing zones are all-important. Only 3 players are allowed in their own defence zone when the puck is outside it. And a player may enter the attacking zone only in line behind the puck or puck carrier. He must not be in the attacking zone when he receives the puck from a player outside it. Any infringement results in a face-off at the nearest face-off point to where the incident took place.

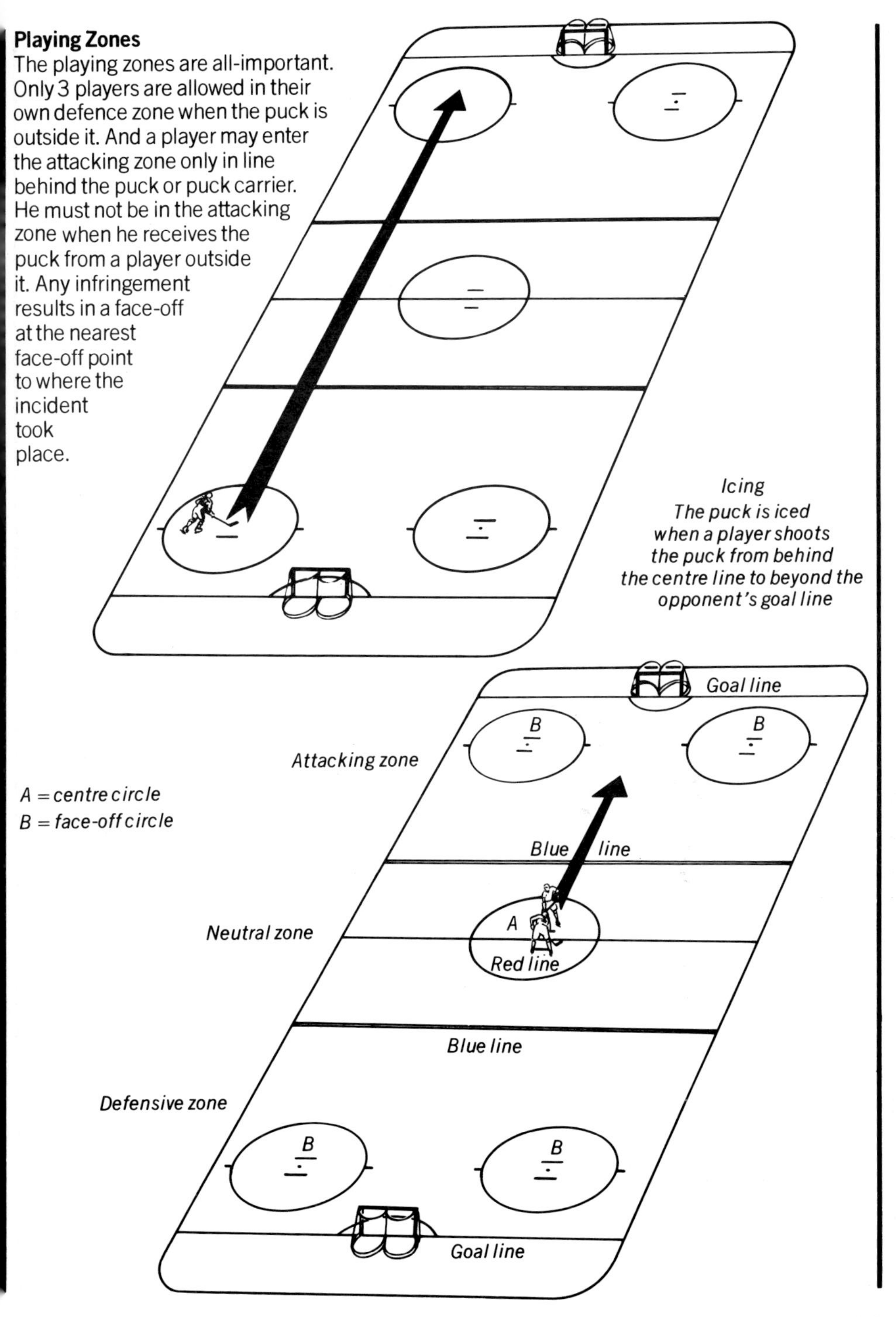

Icing
The puck is iced when a player shoots the puck from behind the centre line to beyond the opponent's goal line

A = centre circle
B = face-off circle

Penalties

One feature of ice hockey is the use of the *sin bin* to which players are sent for various durations depending on the severity of their infringement.

Penalties of 2 minutes are imposed for more minor offences like elbowing, tripping, body checking, playing a high stick. If a goalminder commits a minor offence he does not have to leave the field, but the coach can call off another player instead. If the team with the player advantage score while a player is in the sin bin he can return to the ice immediately the goal is scored.

A major penalty of 5 minutes can be imposed for fighting. When both teams incur major penalties to players they are allowed to be replaced by substitutes. If a goalkeeper commits a major penalty he does not leave the field, but has a penalty shot awarded against him.

A misconduct penalty of 10 minutes can be imposed for the likes of abusive language. But in this case a substitute is allowed to replace the player sent off. A goalkeeper's 'sentence' can be served by a fellow player.

The referee has the power to dismiss from the rink, for the remainder of the game, any player he feels has attempted to deliberately injure another. Although that player takes no further part in the match he may be substituted 5 minutes after his dismissal. A goalminder has to serve his punishment and his place must be taken by another team mate on the ice at that time.

High sticks

Elbowing

Charging

Clothing

Ice hockey player's clothing is specially made for the great safety demands. All players wear knee pads, elbow pads, shin guards, protective shoulder pads, thick padded gloves and special shirts and shorts that give the impression that players are bulkier than they actually are. Helmets are also worn for protection. The goalkeeper looks like something from a science fiction film, and wears a face mask, leather leg-guards, a chest protector and two large, well padded gloves – one for holding the stick and another for catching the puck. Considering the speeds the puck comes at him, the goalkeeper certainly needs this elaborate protection.

Netball

A 7-a-side team game played predominantly by girls and women. Following the invention of basketball in the United States in 1891, American Dr. Toles visited Madame Osterberg's College of Physical Training at Hampstead, London. He taught the students, all young girls, how to play indoor basketball. No rules existed and the 'goals' consisted of 2 waste paper bins. It was from this that netball was developed and rules drawn up.

Object

To score points by putting the ball through the opponents' ring, known as a goal. The team with the most points at the end of the game is the winner.

Duration
Four quarters of 15 minutes each. A 5 minute break is allowed after the 1st and 3rd quarters with a 10 minute break at half time. Teams change ends after each quarter. In some cases, just 2 20 minute halves are played.

Teams
There are 7 players in each team, who take up the following positions: Goalkeeper (GK), Goal Defence (GD), Wing Defence (WD), Centre (C), Wing Attack (WA), Goal Attack (GA), Goal Shooter (GS). The letters in brackets are the ones carried on distinguishing vests worn by the appropriate player.

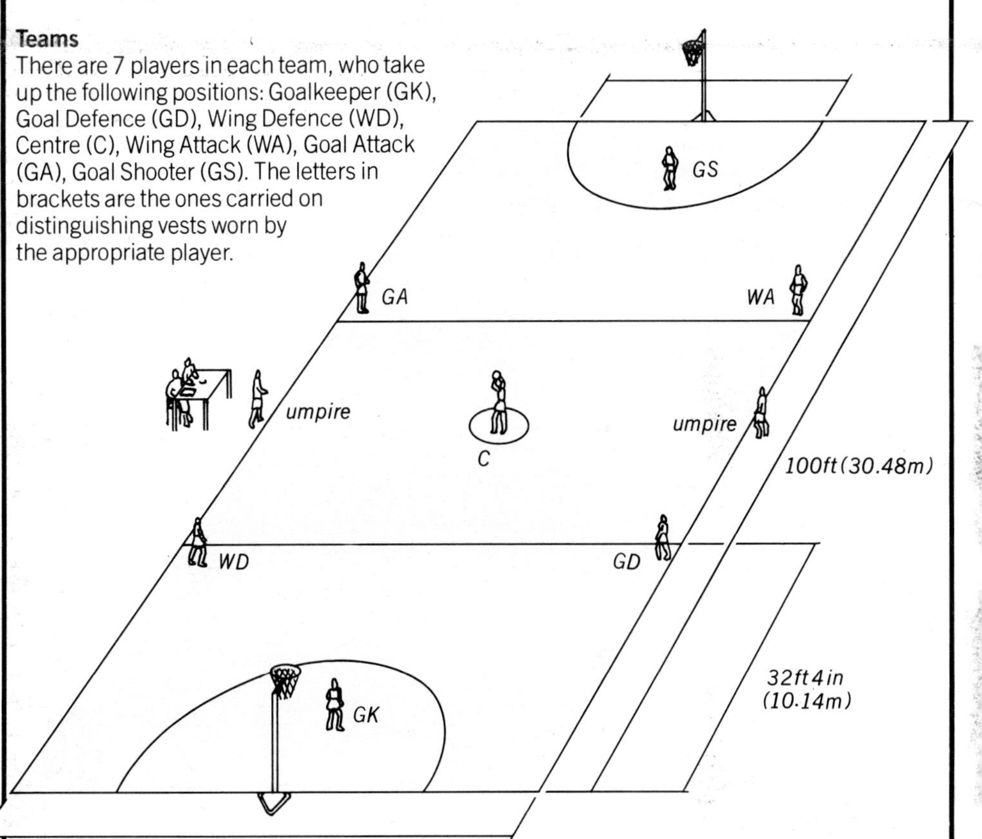

Officials
The game is run by 2 umpires who each control one half of the court, and look after one entire side-line.

Ball
Similar to a size 5 Association Football it is made of leather or of composition and is between 27-28in (68.58-71.12cm) in circumference and 14-16oz (396.9-453.6g) in weight.

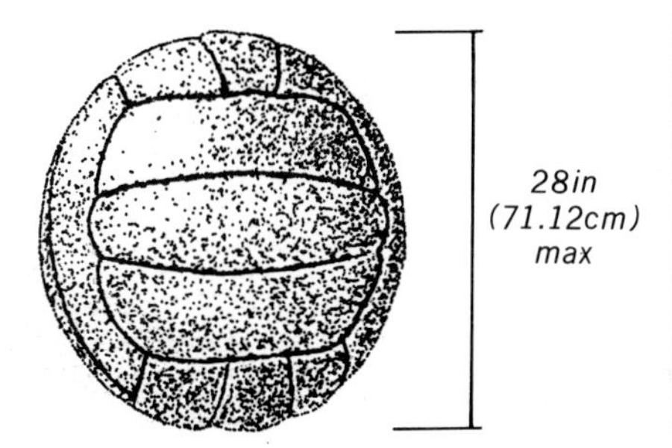

Playing Area

The playing surface should be wooden or concrete. An uneven surface, like grass, is not ideal. The court is 100ft long x 50ft (30.48m x 15.24m) wide and is divided equally into 3 zones – a centre third, and 2 goal thirds. A 3ft (91.44cm) diameter circle is in the middle of the centre and in front of each of the goal posts is a 16ft (4.88m) radius semi-circle. This marks the area of the shooting circle.

The goalposts are situated in the middle of the goal-line. Attached to each at a height of 10ft (3.05m) above the ground, and protruding 6in (15.24cm), there is a 15in (38.1cm) diameter metal ring. A net, open at both ends, is attached to the ring. This is known as the goal.

Offside

Offside has a different meaning in netball than in other sports using the term. Players are restricted to particular areas of the field, and must not venture into another area, or zone.

The plan below shows the court marked into 5 zones and the following is a list of zones each player from one team may enter.

The numbers, of course, are reversed for the opposing team:

Goal Shooter	1 2	Goal Attack	1 2 3
Wing Attack	2 3	Centre	2 3 4
Wing Defence	3 4	Goal Defence	3 4 5
Goal Keeper	4 5		

Any infringement of these rules results in a free pass being given to the opposing team.

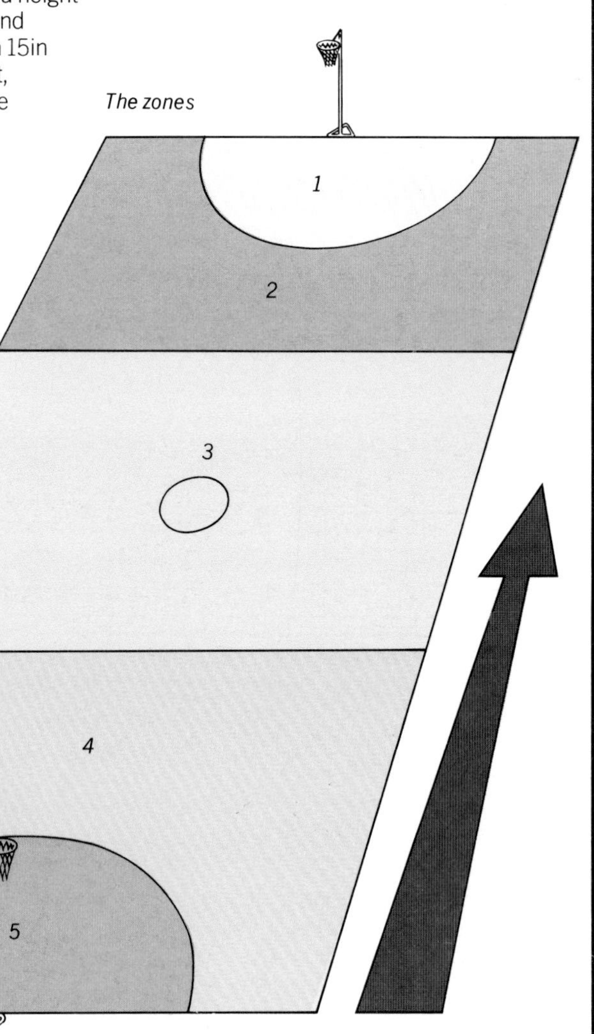

The zones

Starting Play

Play starts, or restarts after a goal or an interval, with a centre pass taken alternately by opposing centres from the centre circle. The centre pass must be caught by another player in the centre third and she must pass the ball within 3 seconds. The object is to get the ball to one of the players allowed to shoot. Only a goal attack or goal shooter is allowed to score, and they must be inside the shooting area. If a defender deflects the ball into the goal as a result of a shot from another player that is also a goal. At least 2 passes must be made before a goal can be scored.

A player must not move with the ball and, although allowed to pivot, must keep one

Pivoting on one foot does not count as a step

foot on the ground. The ball must not be passed over a complete 3rd of the pitch without another player touching it, and no player is allowed within 3ft (91cm) feet of the player with the ball.

A player may catch the ball while in mid-air, land on one foot, and then change

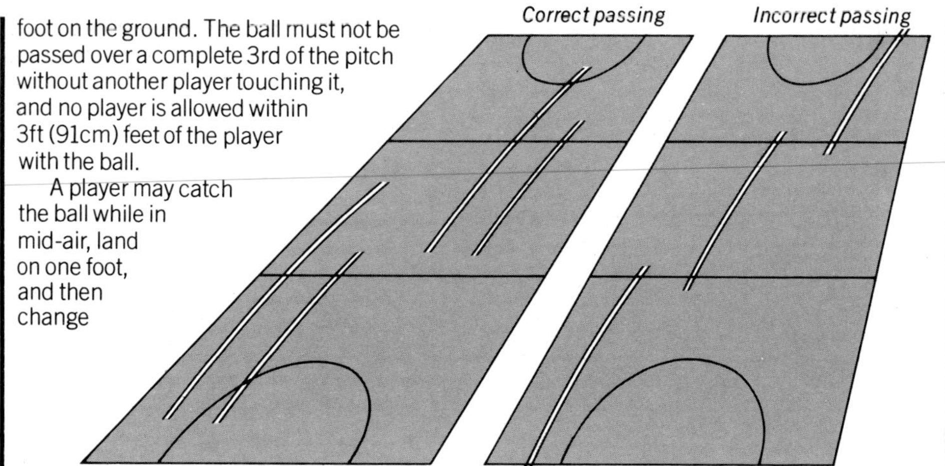

foot in order to pivot. At no time must the ball be rolled, kicked, carried, or thrown to oneself in order to make a double catch.

Throw In
If the ball goes over the side line or goal line play is restarted by a throw in taken by a player from the side who did not last touch the ball, and from the point where it crossed the line.

Obstruction — any player coming closer than 3ft (91cm) to the player with the ball is guilty of obstruction

Clothing
There are no clothing restrictions, except that players must wear' identifying vests so the umpires can make sure they adhere to their correct zones. Footwear must not be spiked.

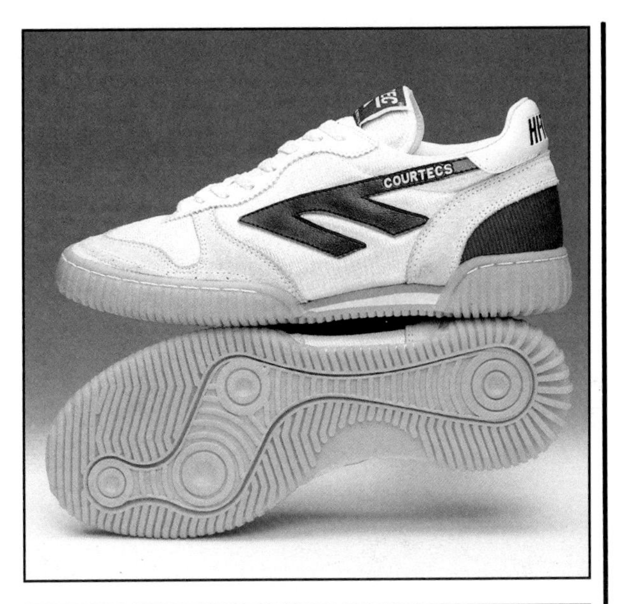

The ring is a steel rod suspended from a post 10ft (3.05m) above the court and fitted with a net open at both ends.

The netball is made of leather, rubber or similar material.

Rugby League

Rugby league is played by 2 teams with 13 players, plus up to 2 substitutes per team. The Rugby League was founded in 1895 as the Northern Union when northern Rugby Union players were refused broken time payments for playing rugby on Saturday afternoons. The new Union allowed for such payments. The rules of the game were the same as Union initially, but over the years many changes have taken place, notably the reduction of players from 15 to 13.

Object
To score points by either scoring tries (placing the ball over your opponent's goal line), or kicking goals by kicking the ball over the crossbar and between the uprights. The team with the most points wins the game.

Duration
Two halves of 40 minutes with a 10 minute break between halves, when the teams swap ends. If play stops because of injury, or any other reason, the referee advises the timekeepers who stop their watches. Extra time is rarely played in Rugby League.

Teams
There are 13 players per team plus up to 2 substitutes. The substitutes may replace a player at any time with the referee's permission and, unlike Association Football, the substituted player may return to the pitch at a later stage as a substitute himself.

Officials
The referee is responsible for enforcing all rules and recording the score. He officiates from the field of play, but is assisted by 2 touch judges who are responsible for one touch line each, covering the length of that line more or less in tandem with each other. They also assist the referee at placed-kicks by standing on the goal line to judge whether the ball has been kicked successfully between the posts. The referee is also helped by 2 timekeepers who stop their watches on the referee's instructions. At the end of 40 minutes actual playing time, one of them sounds a hooter to signal the end of the period.

Ball
The rugby ball is oval shaped and made of leather or a plastic-laminated material. It is fitted with an inflatable bladder. It is $10\frac{3}{4}$-$11\frac{1}{2}$in (27.31-29.21cm) long, between 23-24in (58.42-60.96cm) in circumference at its widest part, and weighs between $13\frac{1}{2}$-$15\frac{1}{2}$oz (382.73-439.43g). Because the ball is frequently kicked out of the ground, many have to be available for use, all of which are inspected by the referee before the start of the game.

Playing Area
The playing area is rectangular and usually grassed, although artificial surfaces have been used. The maximum length of the pitch is 110yd (100m) and the minimum width 60yd (54.86m). The length of the pitch includes the dead-ball area. At each end of

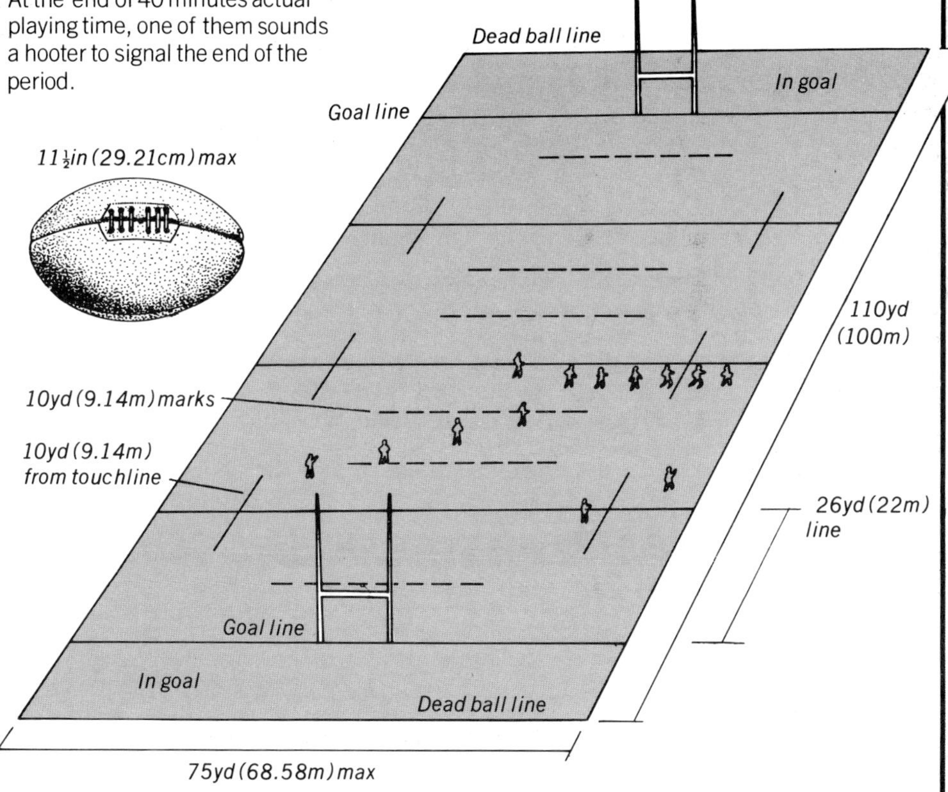

the pitch is a goal 18ft 6in (5.64m) wide. The posts can be any height, but the average is 35-40ft (10.67-12.19m). A crossbar joins the 2 uprights at a height of 10ft (3.05m) above the ground. The bottom of the posts are normally padded to protect the players. A halfway line divides the pitch into 2 halves and a further line is marked 72ft from each goal line. This line is known as the 22-metre line. All 3 dividing lines are marked with a line 10yd (9.14m) in from each touch line. At the back of each goal is a dead-ball line 6-12yd (5.49-10.97m) from the goal line. The area it creates is the in-goal area, where players must attempt to ground the ball to score a try.

Starting Play
The 2 captains toss a coin with the winner taking either kick-off or choice of ends. The player who kicks-off places the ball in the middle of the halfway line and kicks the ball forward. All team mates must be behind him, and all opposing players must be in their own half of the field. The 2nd half starts in the same way, but with the opposing side taking the 1st kick. Each time a point is scored, play is also similarly restarted from the halfway line.

Play and Scoring
Rugby League is a physical contact sport, and players pick up the ball and run with it, pass it or kick it. All passes must be made in a backward direction. Kicks may go forward.

A try is worth 4 points and after each try the scoring team is given a chance to increase their score by having a kick at goal. The kick is taken from a point parallel to the spot where the ball was grounded. It is therefore beneficial to ground the ball between, or as near as possible to, the posts to make the kick that much easier. Defending players must stand behind their own goal line until the kick is made. If the player successfully kicks the ball over the crossbar and between the uprights, 2 more points are added to the score. If the referee awards a penalty, the non-offending team may attempt a place kick at goal from where the incident took place. Again, all opposing players must stand behind their goal line, and a successful kick earns 2 points. A penalty award does not have to result in a player kicking for goal, he can take a tap-kick; in other words tap the ball to himself and carry on play. The other method of scoring points is by the drop-goal. A player can, at any time, attempt to kick the ball over the crossbar from any part of the field by kicking the ball from his hands on the half-volley. A successful kick is worth 1 point.

Try (Grounding the Ball)
A successful try is when a player of the attacking side puts the ball on the ground in the in-goal area. The player does not have to be inside that area, but the ball must be. The ball must be placed *under control,* by the hand, on the goal line or within the in-goal area.

Penalty Try
The referee can, if he feels a player was impeded from scoring a try, award a penalty try to the attacking team. If he does, it is deemed to have been scored between the

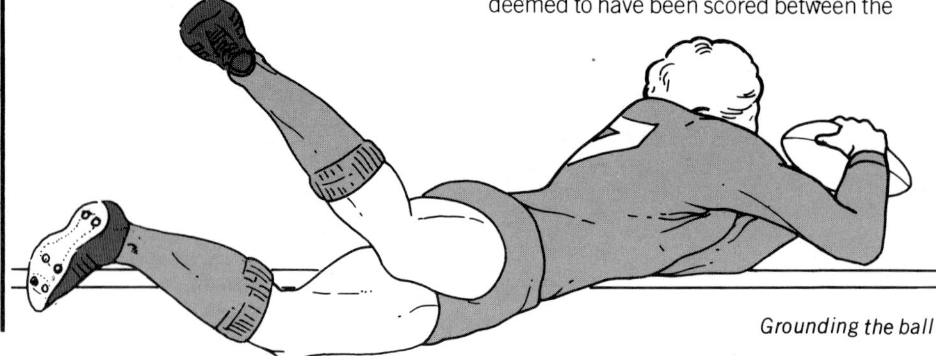

Grounding the ball

posts and the subsequent goal attempt will be from in front of the posts. If a player is fouled in the act of scoring a try the referee has the option of awarding the penalty try, a goal attempt, and a penalty kick, thus creating an '8-point try'.

Tackling

Tackling consists of grasping the opponent in possession of the ball with hands or arms so as to bring him to the floor. The tackle can be made anywhere below the neck. Tackles above the neck are serious offences which often result in dismissal from the field. Tripping is also not allowed. Both those tackles are punishable offences. The basic difference between Rugby League and Rugby Union is that a scrum is not formed after a tackle in the professional game. Once tackled the defending player walks away and the tackled player *plays the ball.* This means he either taps the ball between his legs to a team mate behind, or taps it to himself and restarts his run, thus keeping the game in full flow. Once a team has been tackled 6 times in succession they must release the ball. Normally, before the 6th tackle a player has an attempt at dropping a goal or finding touch by kicking the ball upfield. If a side is tackled a 6th time they automatically lose possession to the opposing side who carry on play and build up their own attack.

Play the ball

At the play the ball one opponent may mark the tackled player; all other team members must stand a distance of at least 5yd (4.57m) away

Out of Play

If a kick goes out of play over the touchline after first bouncing on the field of play, the side who kicked the ball retain possession with a tap kick 10yd (9.14m) in from a point level with where the ball went out. But if the kick leaves the field on the fly without first bouncing, a scrum takes place from the point where the kick was made. An unsuccessful penalty attempt results in the defending team dropping out from their own 22-metre line.

If the ball goes out of play over the defending side's deadball line, and the attacking side was responsible for putting it out, play restarts from the defending team's 22-metre line with either a drop-kick or a tap-kick. If the defending side put the ball out, play resumes with a scrum 5yd (4.57m) from the goal-line. If a player runs over the touchline with the ball, play recommences with a scrum in direct line with the point where he went out of play and 5yd (4.57m) in from the line.

Knock-on

A knock-on is when the ball is propelled towards the opponent's goal line with hand or arm. An infringement is not committed, however, if the offending player gathers the ball before it hits the ground. A knock-on results in a scrum, but, if the referec feels it was deliberate, he can award a penalty. If the opposing side gains an advantage from the knock-on, the referee can allow play to continue.

Offside
A player is offside in open play if he gains possession when in front of a player from his own side who was the last person to touch the ball. Offside also occurs in the play-the-ball situation if a player is within 5yd (4.57m) of the two players involved in the move. If a team kicks the ball upfield and it is gathered by the opposing full backs, any players in front of the kicker may not tackle the full back until he has run at least 16ft 6in (5m). If they do tackle him, they are offside. All offsides are punishable with a penalty.

Scrum
Each side is allowed a maximum of 6 players in the scrum. The ball must be put in cleanly and fairly into the head of the scrum by the appropriate scrum half. The members of the pack must attempt to back heel the ball to their own scrum half who collects the ball and starts an attacking move. There are many scrum offences for which players are penalized, the most important being: *feeding* – when the scrum half deliberately attempts to give his side an advantage with a crooked put-in and *foot up* – when a player attempts to hook the ball too soon.

For scrum offences a *differential* penalty is awarded which means a team can either take a tap kick or kick for touch, and if the latter is found they can take a tap kick from the point where the ball went out of play. The side awarded the scrum is awarded the *head and ball* which means that in addition to throwing the ball into the scrum, the nearest player to the scrum half in the scrum formation is his own prop forward . . . a distinct advantage because he can see the ball coming and be ready.

Knock-on

Sin Bin
Introduced in Britain in 1983, the referee has the power to send a player off the field of play for a specified period of time.

Clothing
The 2 teams must wear contrasting colours, and all players of each team must wear the same coloured shirts, shorts and socks.

Rugby boots are the same as soccer boots. Several players these days like to wear shoulder protection pads, like American Footballers.

High sided Rugby boot

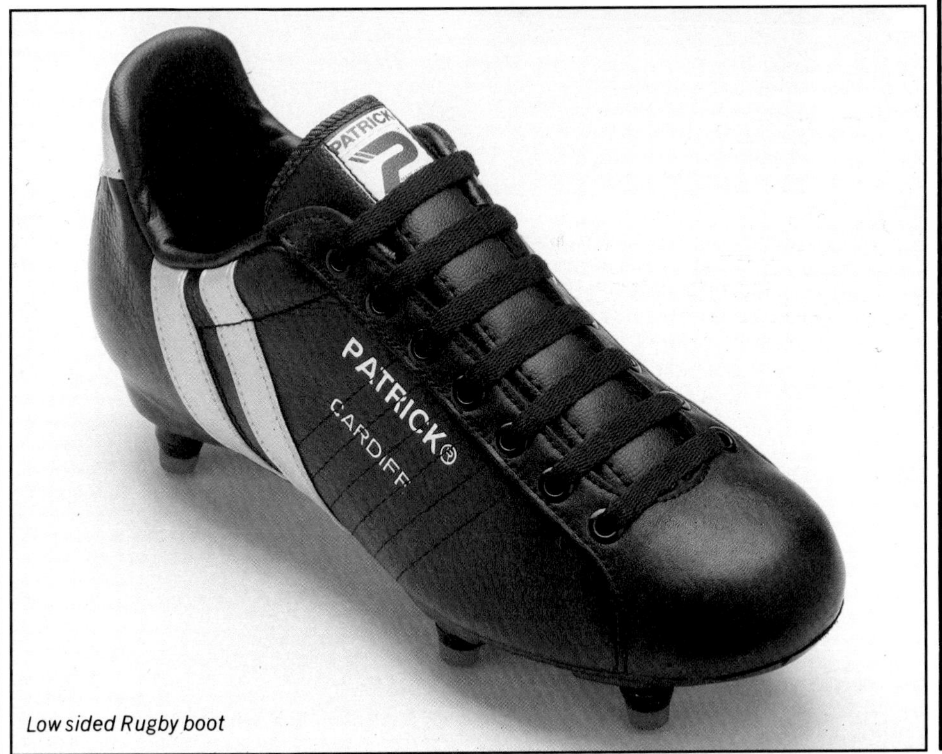

Low sided Rugby boot

Rugby Union

Rugby Union is a ball game played by 2 teams of 15 players, plus up to 2 substitutes (known as replacements).

Rugby is believed to have first been played in 1823 when William Webb Ellis, a student at Rugby school, picked up the ball and ran with it during a game of soccer. It was ten years later that the game started developing in its own right and in 1871, following a meeting at the Pall Mall Restaurant, Cockspur Street, London, on 26 January, the Rugby Football Union was formed.

Object

To ground the ball over your opponents' goal line thus scoring a try, and/or to successfully kick the ball between the uprights and over the crossbar. Tries and goals both score points and the team with the most points wins a game.

Duration

Two halves each of 40 minutes with a 5 minute interval in between. Extra time is rarely played. If scores are level at the end of the match it is a draw. In knock-out competitions the team scoring the most tries in a draw can be declared the winners or, in some cases, the away team.

Teams
There are 15 players in each team with up to 2 substitutes (replacements) allowed only in the case of injury. A team consists of 8 forwards, and 7 backs.

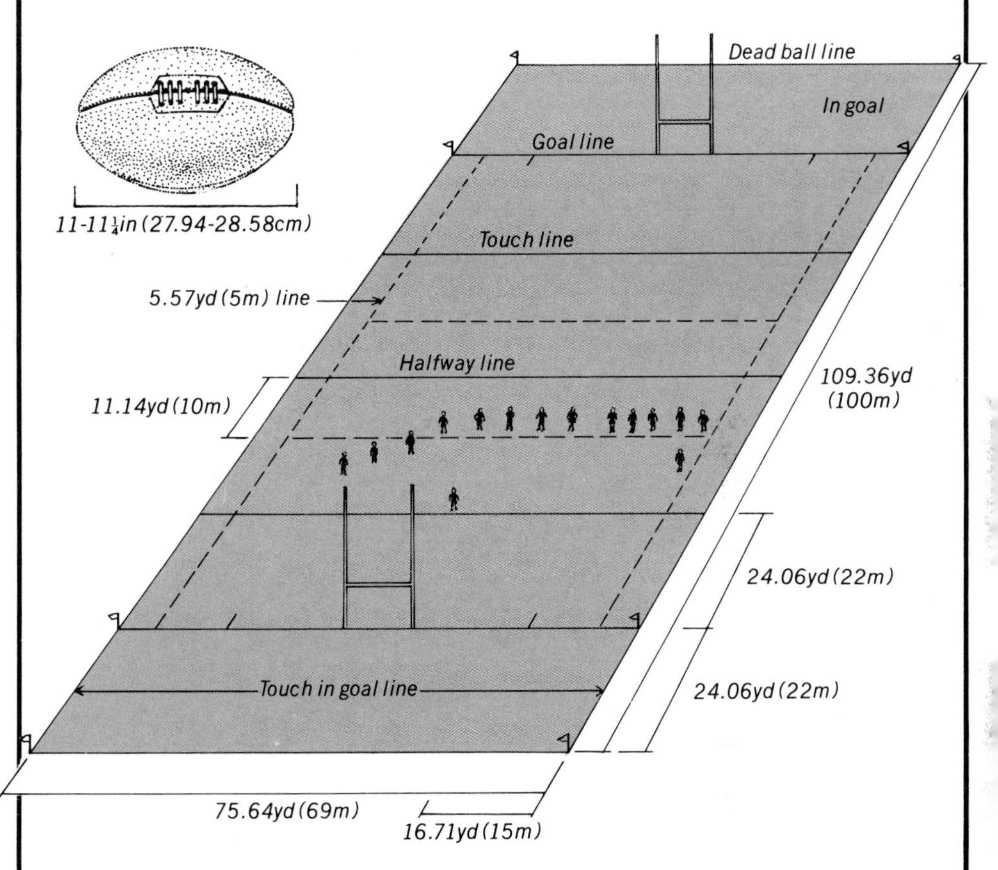

Officials
The referee who records and times the game is the sole judge of fact, and enforces the rules. He is assisted by 2 touch judges who operate down one touchline each. They make decisions on fair play, whether the ball is in or out of play, and assist in advising if a try has been successfully made, or a kick successfully converted.

Ball
Oval and made of leather or other approved material. It is 11-11¼in (27.94-28.58cm) long with a circumference of 30-31in (76.2-78.74cm) from end to end. The circumference at the maximum width should be 24-25½in (60.96-64.77cm). Its weight is between 13½-15oz (382.72-425.25g).

Playing Area
Rugby is played on grass and the maximum dimensions of a pitch are 109.36yd (100m) by 75.64yd (69m). A line 5.57yd (5m) in from each side line (known as the touchline) is drawn the full length of the pitch. The lines at each end of the pitch are known as the goal lines. At a distance of 24.06yd (22m) behind each goal line is the dead ball line. The area in between is the In Goal area and it is in this section that players must score tries. In the middle of each goal line is

a set of goal posts (normally wooden). They are 6.12yd (5.6m) apart and extend to any height, but normally not less than 8.20yd (7.5m). A crossbar joins the 2 posts at a height of 3.28yd (3m) above the ground. A line is drawn across the pitch parallel to the goal line and 24.06yd (22m) in front of it. This is known as the 22m line.

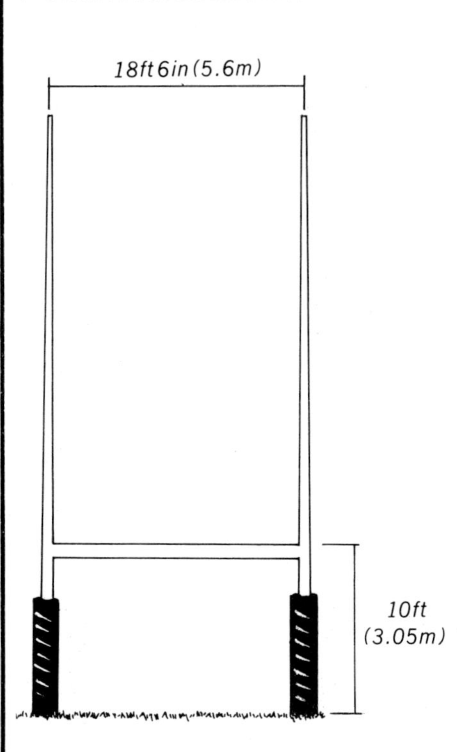

Starting Play

A toss of coin decides which team kicks off. Play starts with the ball placed in the centre of the pitch and kicked towards the opponents' half. Play recommences from a kick in the centre after the scoring of a try or goal.

Once a side has the ball they attempt to get it into opposing territory by (a) carrying it (b) kicking it or (c) passing it. The ball must be passed backwards. If, while carrying the ball, a player is tackled he must release the ball as soon as it hits the ground. Both sets of forwards then form a ruck around the ball and try to heel the ball out to their appropriate scrum half. If such a situation looks like ending in stalemate the referee can award a set scrummage.

If a team scores a try a goal attempt (conversion) automatically follows. This is a place kick at goal taken on the field at a point level with the spot where the touchdown was made. Clearly, then, it is better to score a try as near to the posts as possible.

Scoring

The try is the highest scoring method with 4 points. A conversion of a try is worth 2 more points. A penalty goal taken from a point where an infringement occurs, is worth 3 points, and a drop goal, which may be attempted from anywhere on the pitch, is also worth 3 points. The referee can, at his discretion, award a penalty try if he feels a player was deliberately prevented from scoring a try and, no matter where the infringement occured, the conversion is taken from in front of the posts.

Place kick

Set scrum

The Scrummage

A minimum of 3 players, and maximum of 8 can make up a scrummage (known as the scrum). The front row of the scrum normally consists of 2 props and a hooker. The middle row consists of 2 second row or lock forwards. They are flanked by the 2 wing, or flank, forwards with, on his own at the back of the pack, the No. 8 forward.

The scrum half of the team awarded the scrum puts the ball into the 'tunnel' made by the two sets of front row forwards. As each side pushes against each other, the ball is heeled out of the pack to the scrum half who stands in a position behind the No. 8 forward. No player must lift a foot to the ball until it has properly entered the head of the scrum.

Set scrummages are awarded following minor passing and handling offences. Technical offences at the scrummage and lineout are penalized by a free-kick but an attempt at goal is not permitted. More serious offences result in penalty kicks, which can be made directly at goal.

Lineout

A player may kick the ball directly into touch (over the touchline) without it bouncing providing he is in his own 22m area. If he is outside the area he can still kick into touch but the ball must first bounce on the field of play. In both cases a lineout will take place at a point level with the place where the ball crossed the touchline. If, however, he is outside his 22m area and the ball goes into touch without bouncing, the lineout takes place level with the point from where the kick was taken.

In a lineout at least 2 players per team must line up next to each other and face the player about to throw the ball in from the

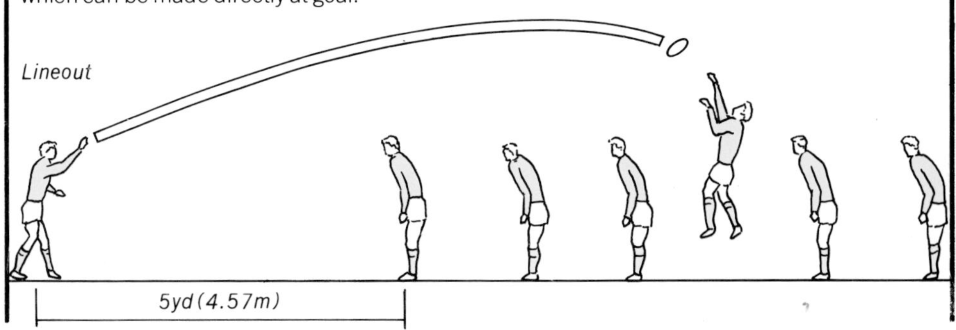

Lineout

touchline. They must maintain their positions – at least 2ft (600mm) apart – until the ball is thrown and then jump and attempt to palm the ball back to a member of their own side.

Offside
A player is offside in general play if he is in front of the ball and attempts to play it after it has been played by a member of his own team. Players can also be offside at lineouts and scrums.

Fouls
It is forbidden to deliberately strike, hack or kick an opponent.
To trip an opponent or make a dangerous tackle with a stiff arm.
To willfully charge or obstruct an opponent who does not have the ball.
Obstruction and deliberate time wasting are penalised by a penalty try or penalty kick. The referee has the discretion to caution and /or dismiss players for infringements of the laws and spirit of the game.

Obstruction
It is forbidden to impede an opponent who does not have the ball

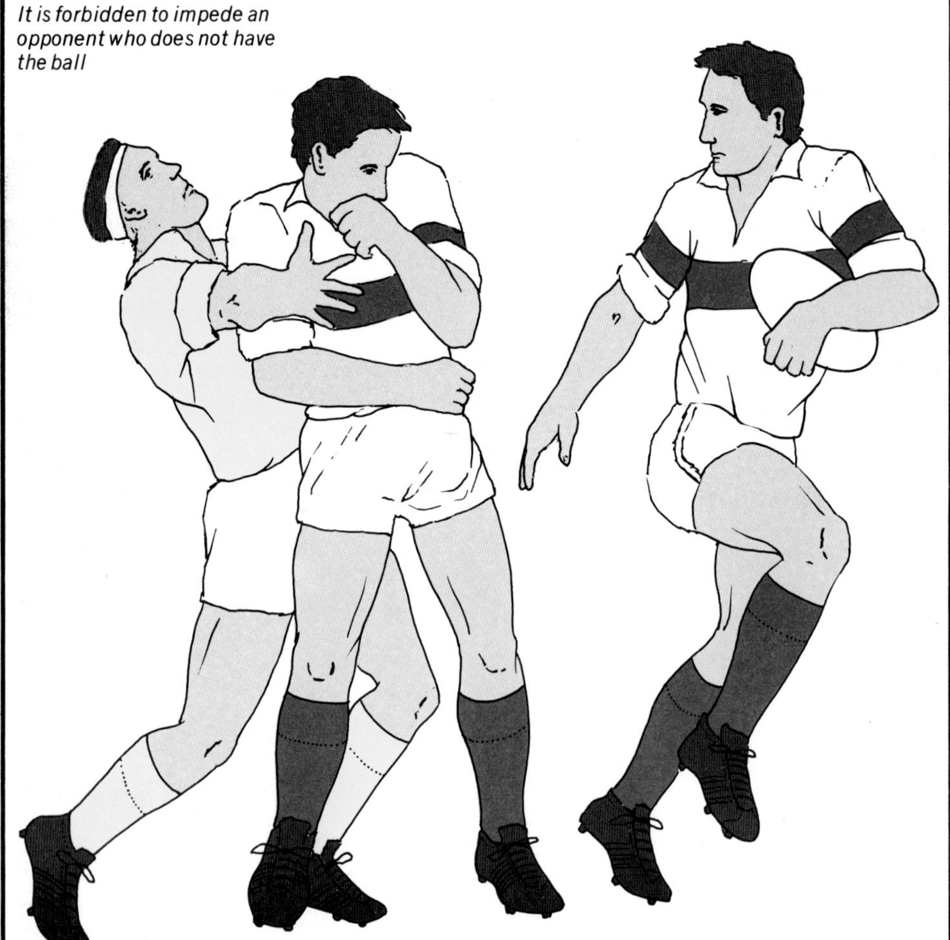

Clothing
Clothing is the same as that for Rugby League, illustrated on page 107.
Teams wear the same colour shirts, shorts and socks. Rugby boots are slightly bigger than soccer boots and have built up ankle areas with padded protection. Some rugby players wear protective shoulder pads.

Snooker

Snooker is an indoor game played by 2 players, as individuals, or by 4 players, as doubles.

Object
To win more frames than your opponent(s) in any single game.

Duration
A game consists of a pre-determined number of frames and can consist of as few as 1. There is no restriction on the maximum number of frames, but, as a guide, the Embassy World Professional Championship final is played over 35 frames.

Scoring
To win a frame you must score more points than your opponent(s). Points are scored by making breaks which build as a result of potting, alternately, a red ball followed by 1 of the 6 coloured balls. As each red is potted, it remains in the pocket, but the coloured balls are returned to the table and placed on their appropriate spot. When all the red balls have been potted the coloured balls have to be potted in ascending order as follows: yellow-green-brown-blue-pink-black. Players take turns to attempt to establish a break, which comes to an end when a player fails to pot a ball, or commits a foul.

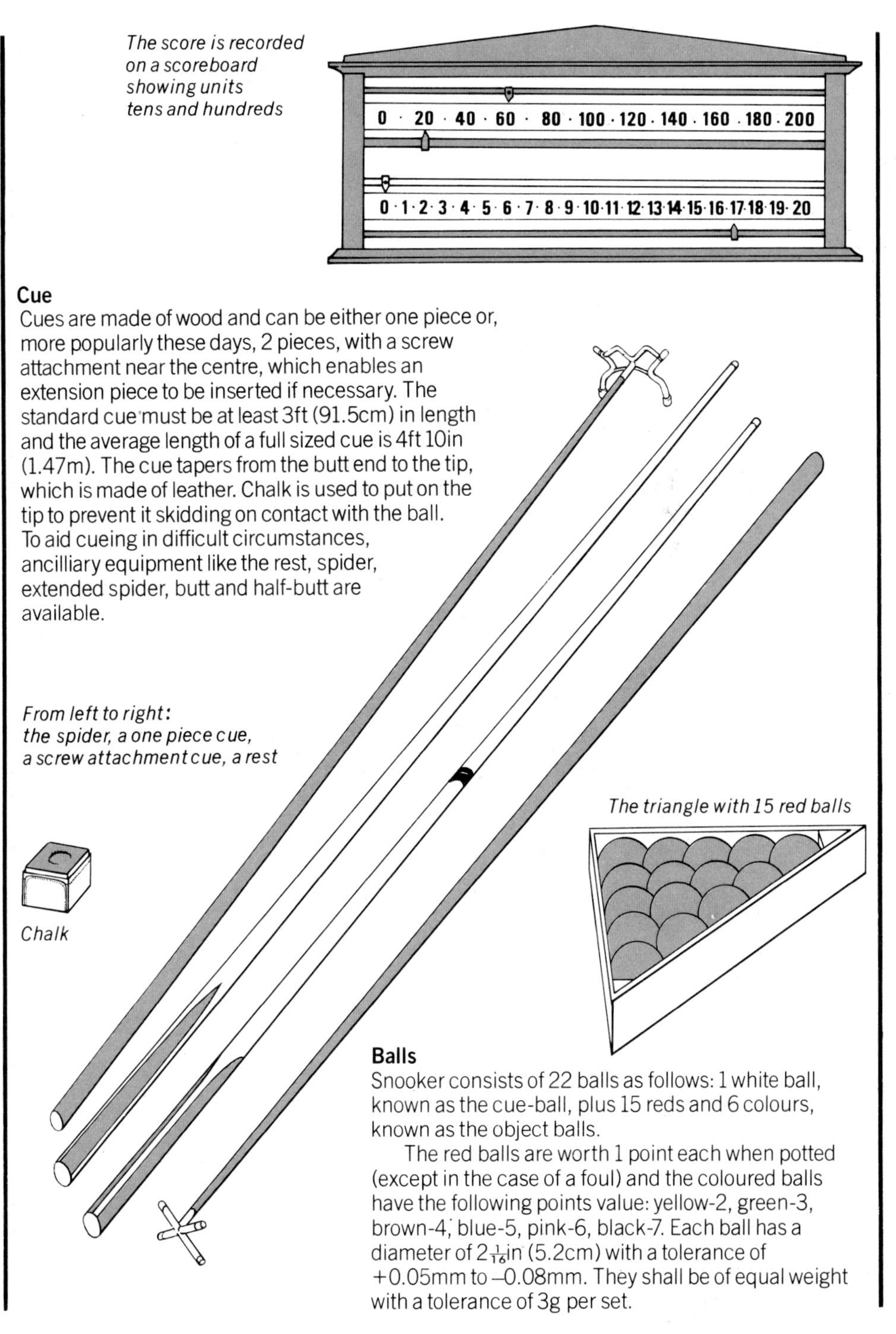

The score is recorded on a scoreboard showing units tens and hundreds

Cue

Cues are made of wood and can be either one piece or, more popularly these days, 2 pieces, with a screw attachment near the centre, which enables an extension piece to be inserted if necessary. The standard cue must be at least 3ft (91.5cm) in length and the average length of a full sized cue is 4ft 10in (1.47m). The cue tapers from the butt end to the tip, which is made of leather. Chalk is used to put on the tip to prevent it skidding on contact with the ball. To aid cueing in difficult circumstances, ancilliary equipment like the rest, spider, extended spider, butt and half-butt are available.

From left to right: the spider, a one piece cue, a screw attachment cue, a rest

Chalk

The triangle with 15 red balls

Balls

Snooker consists of 22 balls as follows: 1 white ball, known as the cue-ball, plus 15 reds and 6 colours, known as the object balls.

The red balls are worth 1 point each when potted (except in the case of a foul) and the coloured balls have the following points value: yellow-2, green-3, brown-4, blue-5, pink-6, black-7. Each ball has a diameter of $2\frac{1}{16}$in (5.2cm) with a tolerance of +0.05mm to –0.08mm. They shall be of equal weight with a tolerance of 3g per set.

Table

Snooker is played on a standard English billiard table which has a playing area, within the cushion faces, of 11ft 8$\frac{1}{2}$in (3.56m) x 5ft 10in (1.78m). The height of the table from the floor to the top of the cushion rail is between 2ft 9$\frac{1}{2}$in (85.2cm) and 2ft 10$\frac{1}{2}$in (87.2cm). The bed of the table is made of slate and covered in a stretched cloth. The cloth is marked with 6 spots, each of which is the home of one of the coloured balls. The area between the yellow, green and brown spots, and the end cushion nearest them is known as the baulk area. The cushions are vulcanized rubber. The cushion at the baulk end of the table is known as the bottom cushion. There are 2 pockets at either end of this cushion. The cushion at the opposite end of the table is known as the top cushion and the 2 pockets at the end of it are the top pockets. There are also 2 pockets at the middle of the table. The rules of snooker do not stipulate the width of the pockets, they only state they must conform to standard templates. But, as a rule, the width is approximately 3$\frac{1}{2}$in (8.9cm).

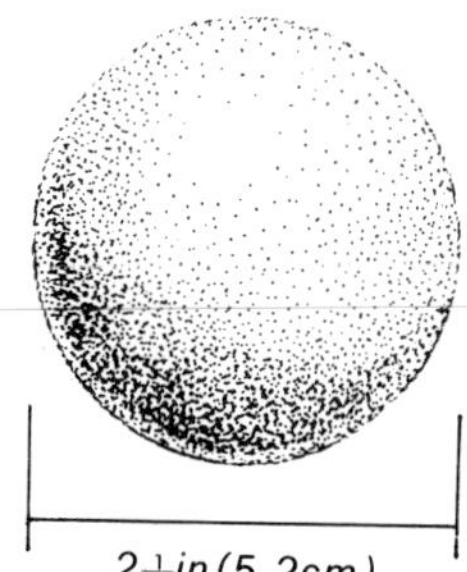

Starting
After tossing a coin to decide the order of play, the first player places the cue-ball within the 'D' area of the table and aims to make contact with 1 or more of the reds. If he pots a red, scoring 1 point, he then nominates a colour. If he pots that, the value is added to the 1 point gained for potting the red, and so on until his break comes to an end. The opposing player then comes to the table and attempts to pot balls if he so wishes – he does NOT have to attempt a pot, but he must make contact with the appropriate object ball. He may, if he feels he cannot pot a ball, *snooker* his opponent. In other words, place the cue-ball in such a position that the opponent does not have clear access to the object ball(s) which are *on*. A ball is said to be *on* when it is the next ball intended to be hit. If, after all the balls have been potted, the scores are level, the black ball is re-spotted. The players again toss to decide who plays first, and play re-commences with the cue-ball in the 'D'.

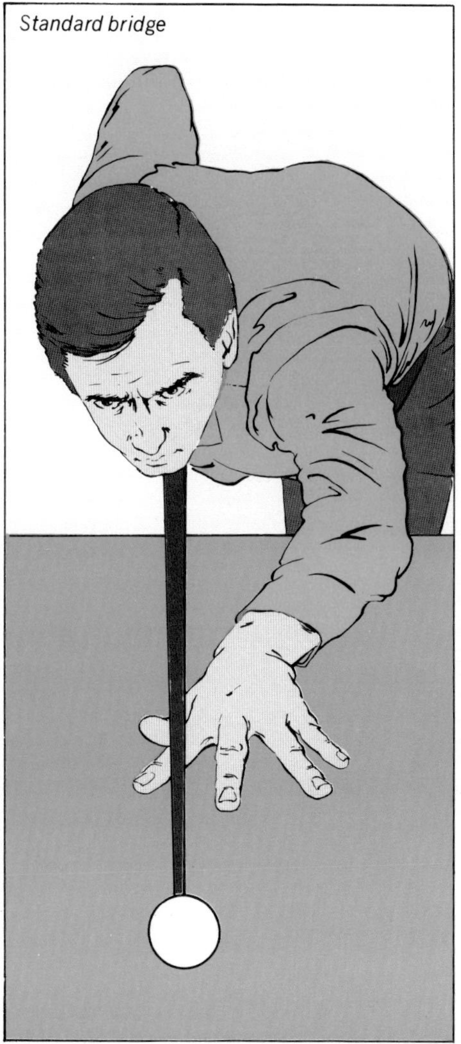
Standard bridge

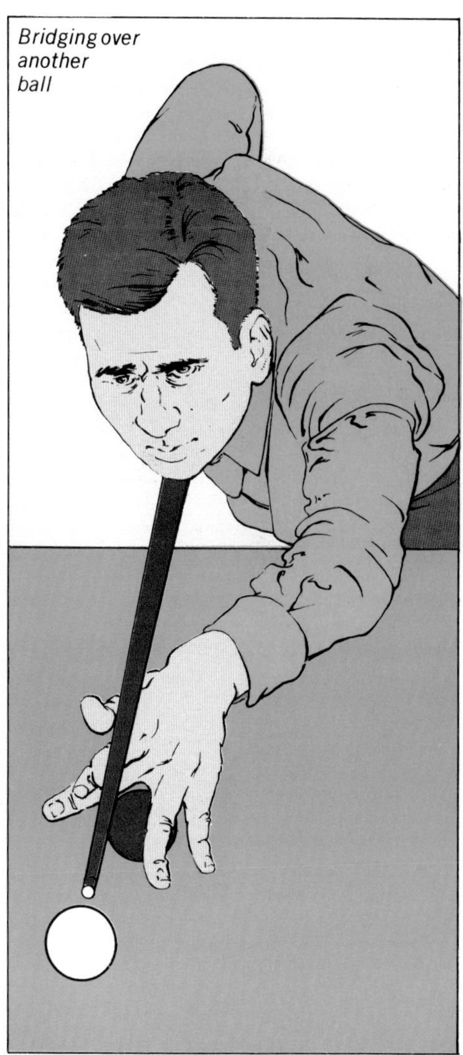
Bridging over another ball

Fouls

There are many ways in which fouls can be committed. The most common are:
1 Failing to hit the object ball
(Penalty points added to your opponent's score: the points value of the ball on, subject to a minimum penalty of 4 points.)
2 Putting the white ball in the pocket
(Penalty: as above.)
3 Hitting the wrong ball or causing the wrong ball to enter the pocket
(Penalty: value of the ball hit or value of the ball on whichever is the greater. Subject to the usual minimum of 4 points.)

Other fouls that incur penalties subject to the value of the ball on or concerned are:

- Playing when the balls are not at rest
- Hitting the cue-ball more than once
- Playing with both feet off the floor – at least 1 foot must be on the floor
- Playing out of turn
- Forcing a *snooker* after a *free-ball*
- Causing the cue-ball to jump over the object ball
- Playing a push stroke, i.e. when the tip of the cue is still in contact with the cue-ball after it has started its forward motion or, while it is making contact with an object ball
- Forcing a ball off the table
- Touching a ball other than with the tip of the cue
- Striking the cue-ball when a coloured ball is incorrectly spotted

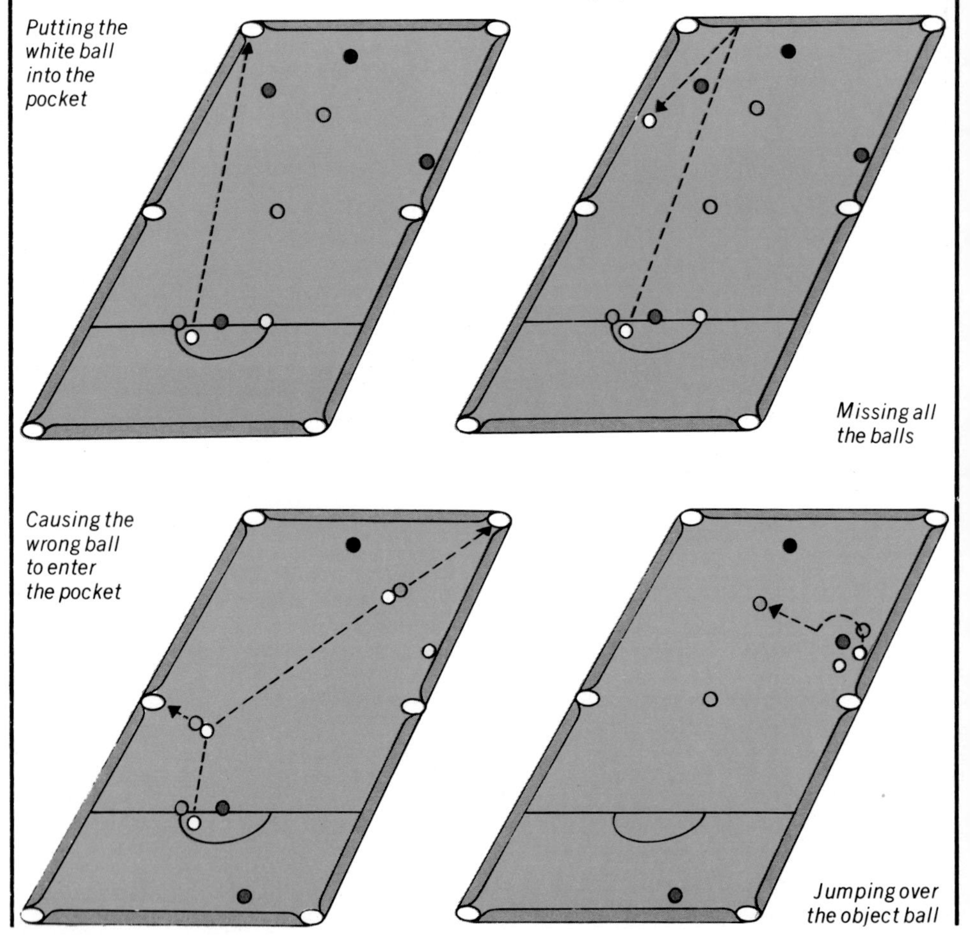

Putting the white ball into the pocket

Missing all the balls

Causing the wrong ball to enter the pocket

Jumping over the object ball

Snooker
The cue ball is snookered when it is impossible to make a direct stroke in a straight line to any part of every ball that is 'on'. The word snooker itself was used to describe new recruits at the Royal Military Academy at Woolwich. During a game of billiards at Jubbulpore, India, in 1875 General Sir Neville Chamberlain called a fellow officer a snooker after he had missed an easy pot. The term stuck.

snooker

Free Ball
If a player is *snookered* after his opponent has committed a foul that player can either make his opponent play again or take a free ball. If he chooses the latter he can pot any ball on the table and count its score as if it was the ball on. If the ball on was a red he may, for example pot the brown, which would count as 1 point, then he would continue his break in the normal manner by next potting a colour.

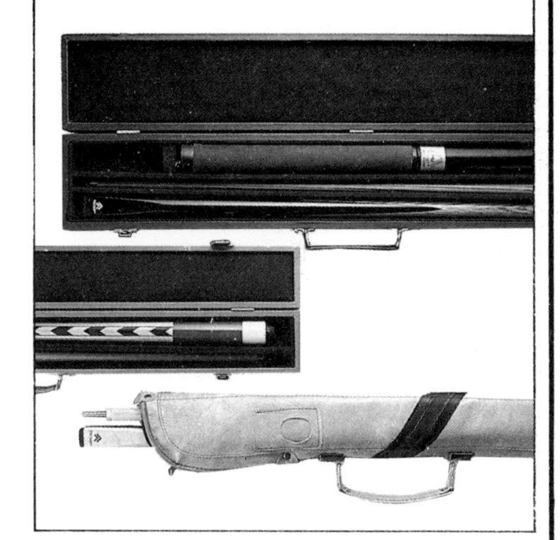

Clothing
While professional players must, by the rules of their Association, wear morning suits for afternoon play in tournaments, and evening dress for the evening's session, there are no rules laid down for the non-professional players. But most clubs like to see the well dressed image of the game maintained, even at grass roots level.

Modern cues are made of Canadian maple and South American hard woods like ebony and rosewood. The two-piece cue was introduced in the 1970's and John Spencer won the 1977 world title using one.

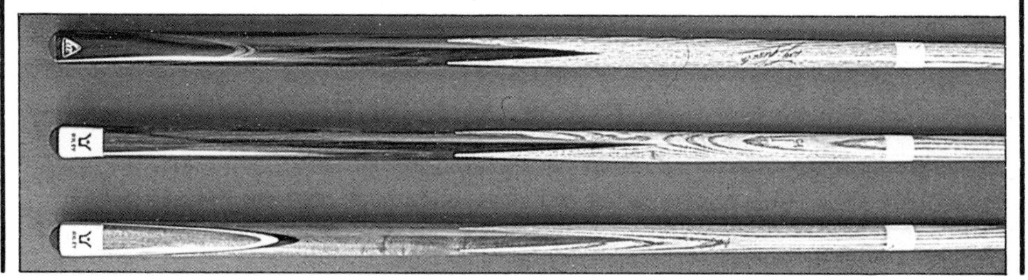

Soccer

Soccer, in some form or other, has been played for thousands of years and it is probable that the first international match was between the ancient Greeks and Chinese. Soccer was certainly played in the Middle Ages but a succession of monarchs, led by Edward II in 1314, banned the game because it hindered archery and other martial arts. The first set of soccer rules were drawn up at Cambridge University in 1846 and 17 years later the Football Association was formed. The Football League was inaugurated in 1888 and the world governing body, FIFA, was founded in 1904.

Soccer (Association Football)
Soccer is a ball game played by 2 teams with 11 players, plus up to 2 substitutes per team.

Object
To score more goals than the opposing team. If both teams score the same number of goals, the game is declared a draw. Some competitions make allowance for extra time and a penalty shoot-out at the end to establish a winner.

27-28in (68-71cm)

Ball

Made of leather or other approved material, the ball is round with a circumference of 27-28in (68-71cm). Its weight should be between 14-16oz (396-453g) and it should be inflated to a pressure of 15lb/sq. in (1kg/sq. cm). The referee must inspect the ball before the start of play, and it must not be changed during a match without his permission.

The referee

Duration

A game consists of 2 equal halves, each lasting 45 minutes. There is a 10 minute interval between halves. When play is halted because of injury to a player, the referee should stop his watch and this time is added to the end of the appropriate half.

If the rules of a competition order extra time to be played when a result has not been determined at the end of 90 minutes, 2 further periods, each of 15 minutes, with a 5 minute interval in between, are played.

Teams

The names of the 11 players and substitute(s) must be handed to the referee in good time before the match, and one of the 11 players must be a goalkeeper. A substitute may replace another player at any time, providing he has the referee's permission to enter the field. The player replaced may not re-enter the field of play. A substitute cannot replace a player dismissed from the field.

Officials

A referee has ultimate control over the game and it is his job to time the match, record the scores, and make sure the rules are enforced. He is assisted by 2 linesmen, each controlling one half of the field. Their job is to advise when the ball is out of play, and to award throw-ins and goal-kicks. They also guide the referee on matters of off-side or any other infringement of the laws. The clothing of the officials should not clash with either team; normally they wear black.

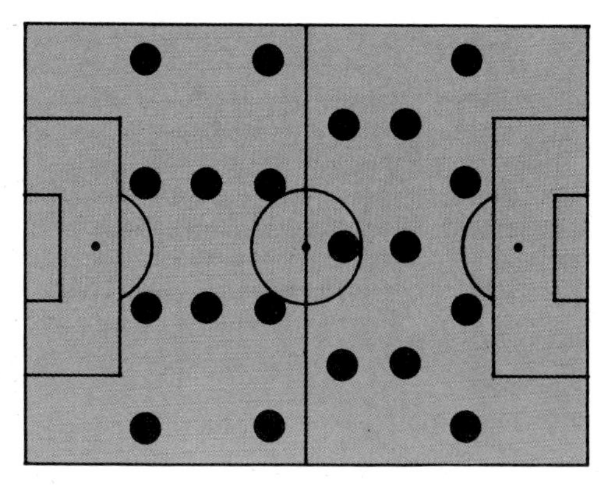

4-2-4 Formation *4-3-3 Formation*

Playing Area
Soccer is played on a rectangular area, normally grass, although some modern pitches are synthetic. The width of a pitch must be 50-100yd (45-90m) and its length must be between 100-130yd (90-120m).

The playing area is divided into 2 equal halves by a centre line in the middle of which is a centre spot, from which is drawn a circle (known as the centre circle) with a radius of 10yd (9.15m).

At each end of the pitch is a goal, positioned in the middle of the end line, known as the goal line. The goal is 8yd (7.32m) wide and 8ft (2.44m) high. A net is attached to the back of the wooden goal framework.

A goal area 20yd (18.32m) x 6yd (5.5m) is marked on the pitch in front of each goal. That area is within a larger penalty area which is marked on the pitch. The penalty area is 44yd (40.32m) x 18yd (16.5m). At a point 12yd (11m) from, and perpendicular to, the goal line is marked a penalty spot. In the middle of the longest edge of the penalty area is scribed an arc (but outside the area) with a 4yd (3.66m) radius. The arc exists to ensure all players are at least 10yd (9.14m) from the ball when a penalty kick is taken.

In all 4 corners of the playing area there is a corner flag on a stick which must be a minimum 5ft (1.5m) high. At the corner is an arc indicating the corner area. This arc has a radius of 1yd (1m).

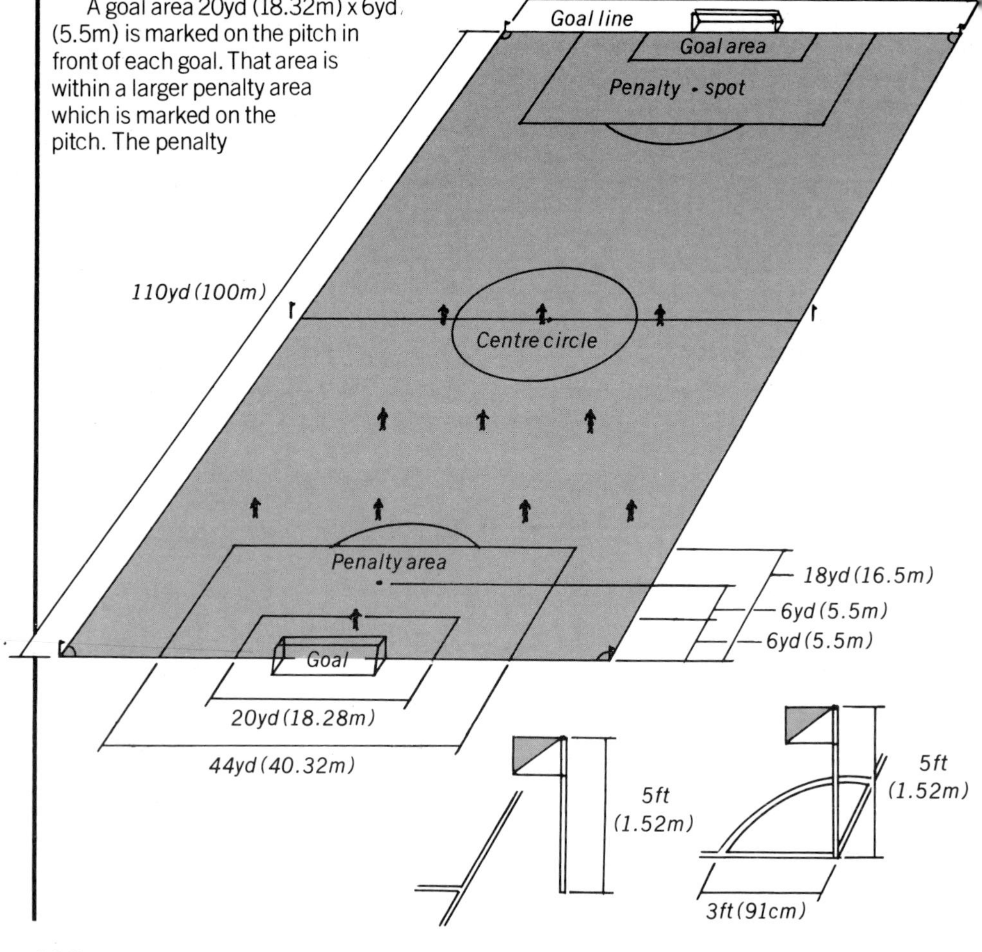

Starting Play
The 2 captains toss a coin to decide whether they choose which end to defend, or whether they kick-off. When the referee is satisfied that all players are in their own half of the field, play commences from a stationary position on the centre spot. A player from one team kicks off, moving the ball its own circumference. All players from the opposing team must be outside the centre circle at the start of play. Once a player has set the ball in motion he must not touch it again until another player has.

When a goal is scored play recommences from the centre spot, with the team who conceded the goal kicking off. For the 2nd half, the teams change ends and the opposite team kicks off.

Playing the Ball
The ball must be kicked or headed, or played with any part of the body other than the arms or hands (with the exception of the goalkeeper or when taking a throw-in).

Although the goalkeeper is allowed to handle the ball, he may only do so within the confines of the penalty area (excluding the arc), and once he has touched the ball with his hand is allowed only 4 steps before releasing the ball. A goalkeeper may

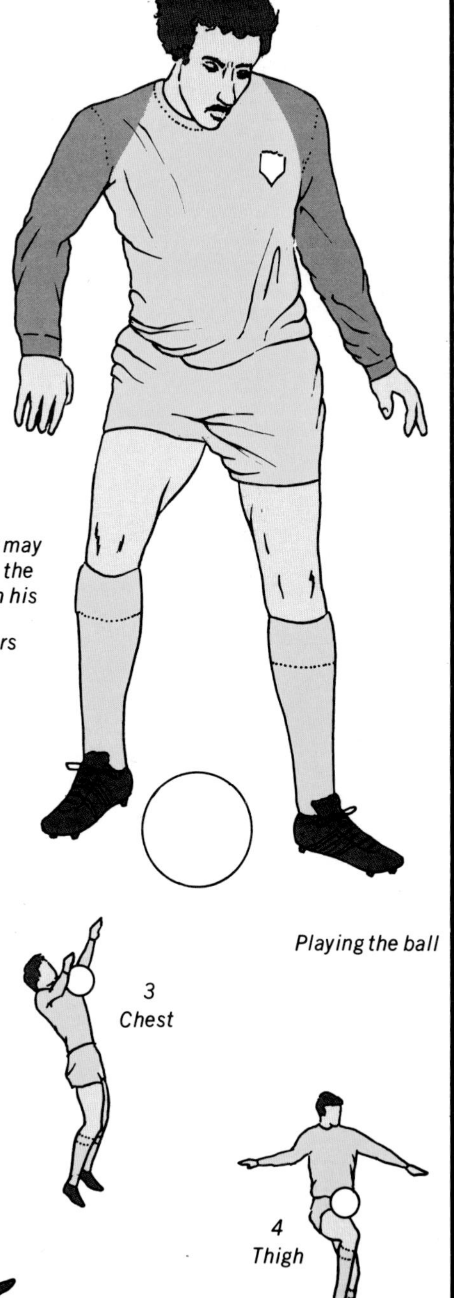

A player may not play the ball with his arms or shoulders

Playing the ball

play the ball outside the penalty area, but must not use his hands.

If the ball hits an outfield player's hand or arm, the referee has to decide whether it was deliberate or accidental. If deliberate, he awards a free kick to the opposing team.

Scoring
A goal is scored when the WHOLE of the ball crosses the line, and the team scoring has not infringed any rules in the process.

Out of Play
The ball is out of play when the ENTIRE ball crosses the line, marking the perimeter of the field of play.

If the ball crosses the longer line (the side-line) a throw-in is awarded against the team whose player last touched the ball. If the ball crosses the goal line it is either a goal-kick or corner-kick, depending on which player last played the ball. If it was a defending player, a corner-kick is awarded; if an attacking player, a goal-kick.

Throw-In
The throw is taken from the spot where the ball crossed the side line. The thrower must hold the ball with both hands and deliver the ball from behind and over his head. He must be facing the field of play and have at least part of each foot on the ground. He must not touch the ball after taking the throw until another player has touched it. A goal cannot be scored direct from a throw-in.

Goal-Kick
The kick (normally taken by the goalkeeper) is taken from inside the goal area in the half of the area nearest to where the ball went out of play. The ball is not in play again until it has left the penalty area. A goal cannot be scored direct from a goal-kick.

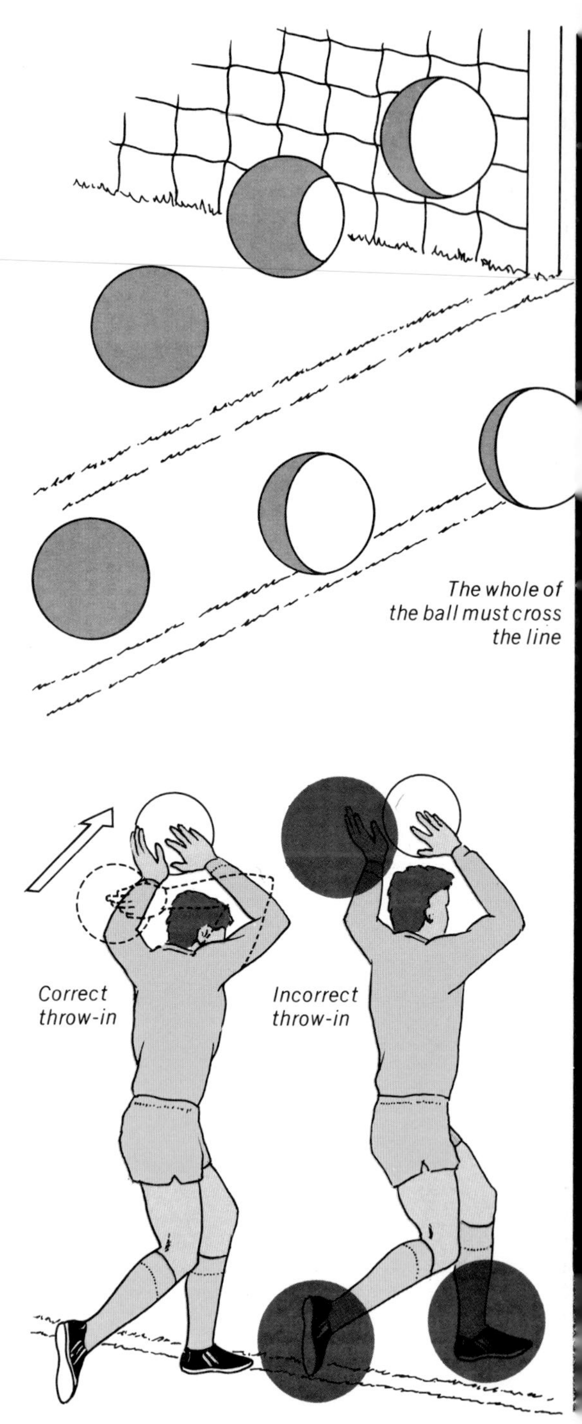

The whole of the ball must cross the line

Corner-Kick
The ball must be placed entirely in the quarter circle near the corner flag and must be kicked by an attacking player. The defending team must stand at least 10yd (9.15m) away from the ball. A goal can be scored direct from a corner-kick.

Penalty-Kick
A penalty kick is awarded for a direct free kick offence which occurs within the penalty area. The only players allowed inside the penalty area at the time of a penalty-kick are the goalkeeper and the player taking the kick. All other players must remain outside the area until the kick is taken. The goalkeeper must stand upright on his goal line and must not move until the kick is taken. The kicker cannot pass the ball to himself, and he cannot touch the ball again until another player has touched it. He cannot hit a ball into the goal that rebounds off the upright.

If the goalkeeper moves, or a defending player enters the penalty area before the ball is kicked, the referee can order the kick to be retaken if unsuccessful. If a member of the attacking team enters the area before the kick is taken, and it is successful, he can also order it to be re-taken.

The referee must allow time for the penalty to be taken if the end of normal time has arrived but, once the kick has been taken and the ball is saved or hits an upright, the kick is deemed to have been concluded.

If the rules of a competition demand a penalty shoot-out at the end of normal play each side takes 5 penalties, by 5 different players, and the team that converts the most is the winner. If the scores are still level the shoot-out continues on a sudden-death basis until a winner is found.

Free-Kicks
After a foul has been committed, the referee awards a free-kick. The nature of the offence decides whether it is a direct, or indirect free-kick. In both cases the offending team must stand 10yd (9.15m) from the ball. If the kick is direct the ball can legitimately enter the goal without touching another player. If indirect, the ball must touch another player before entering the net before a goal can be awarded. An indirect free-kick can be awarded in the penalty area, but a direct free-kick offence inside the area is punished with a penalty.

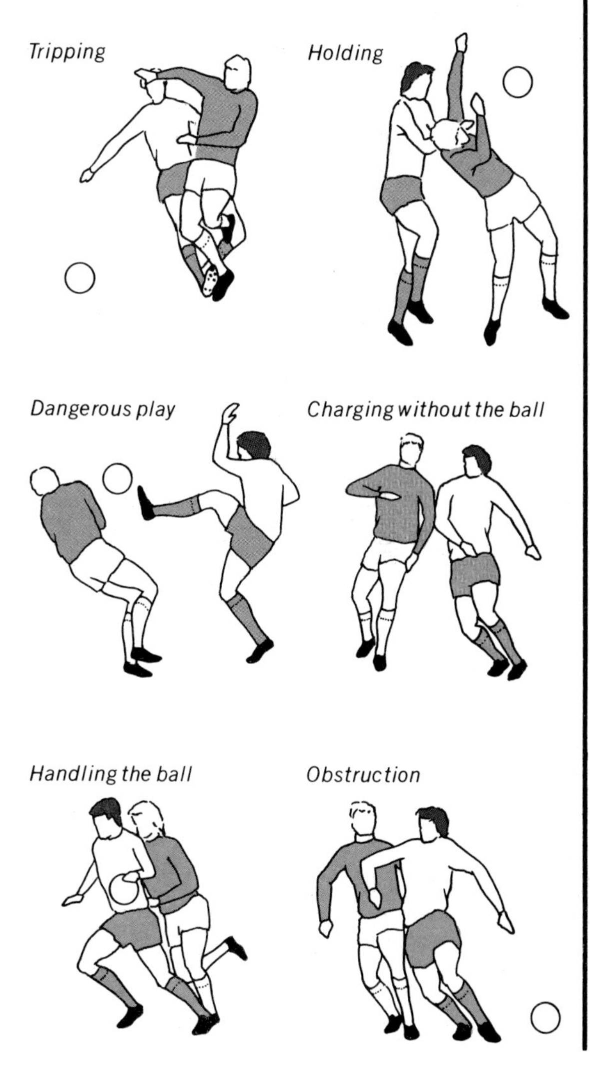

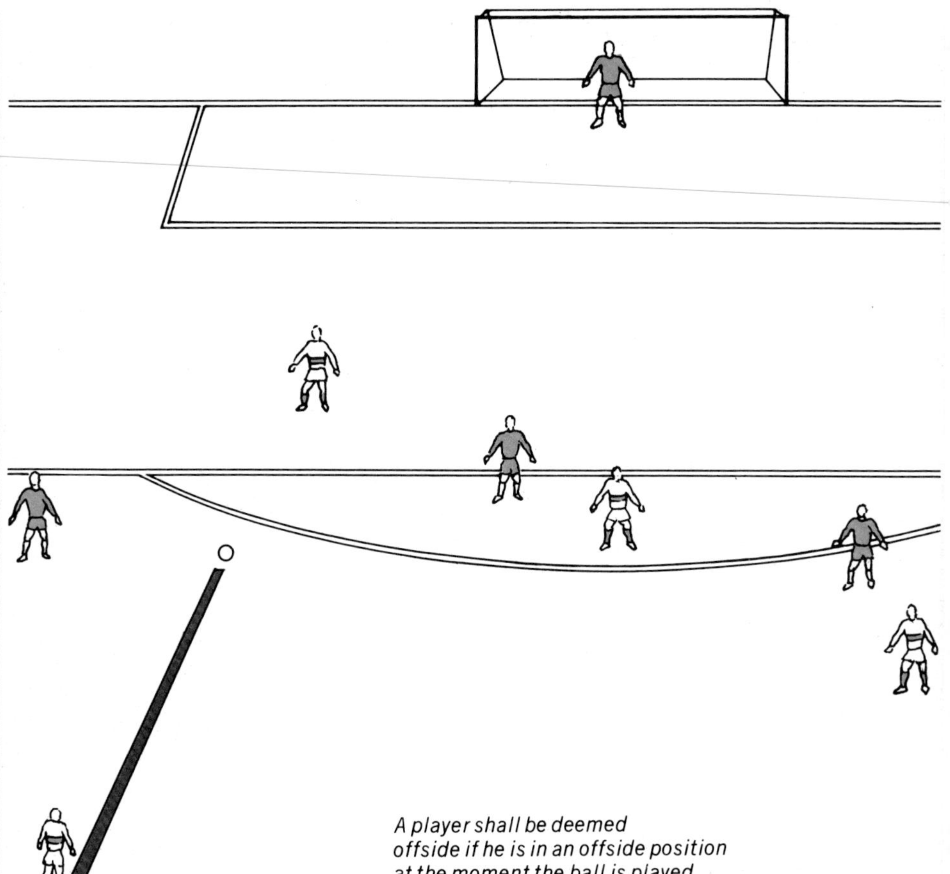

A player shall be deemed offside if he is in an offside position at the moment the ball is played

Offside

A player is in an offside position if he is nearer to his opponents' goal-line than the ball unless:

He is in his own half of the field or there are at least 2 of his opponents nearer their own goal-line than he is.

A player shall be deemed offside if he is in an offside position at the moment the ball is played by one of his own team and he is, in the opinion of the referee, interfering with play. A player cannot be offside if he receives the ball direct from a throw-in, goal-kick, or corner-kick. An offside offence is punishable with an indirect free-kick.

World class goalkeepers like England's Peter Shilton use gloves in wet conditions to improve their grip on the ball. Some goalkeepers wear them all the time, to protect their fingers, particularly when punching clear.

England's new strip . . . just what every Soccer mad schoolboy wants. But don't forget the shin pads, now lightweight but super strong.

The first footballs were blown up pigs' bladders booted around the farmyard. Now they are super-sophisticated, made in smooth leather panels over a snug fitting lace-less inner tube.

Football boots have become increasingly lightweight with the introduction of plastic uppers and soles as well as leather. Plastic screw in studs come in several lengths to suit different conditions.

PATRICK
PLATINI EURO
PUMA
SCHEMER
PUMA
DALGLISH-HATTRICK
WEST GERMANY
NIKE
DIVISION
mitre
SIROCCO

Squash

An indoor bat and ball game which, because of the restrictive playing area is normally played by only 2 people at a time. Doubles play is possible, but a great deal of tolerance is required. The boys of Harrow School are said to be the first to have played squash. Waiting to play rackets, they hit a ball in a smaller area and, because of the confined space, used a soft rubber ball, one which could be *squashed*. Squash became popular with the wealthy, who built squash courts adjacent to their large houses. The Squash Rackets Association was formed in 1929.

Object

To obtain more points than your opponent by winning rallies.

Duration

There is no time limit to a match, which normally consists of the best-of-3 or 5 games. Each game is played until one player reaches 9 points. However, like Badminton, a player may *set* the match if the scores are level at 8-8. The first player to reach 8 may decide to carry on until one of them reaches 10 points. If he does not exercise that right, the game ends when one player reaches 9 points.

Players
The biggest hazard in squash is players running into each other. Rallies are replayed if players hit or obstruct each other accidentally. If it is felt such an action was deliberate then the referee has the power to award a penalty point against the offender. Players must at all times make every effort to get out of their opponent's way.

Officials
Play is controlled by an off-court referee who ensures all rules are maintained. But his most important role is to make decisions on accidental or deliberate baulking. He is also responsible for calling out the score, always starting with that of the server. When service changes hands he states *'Hand-out'* and then the score.

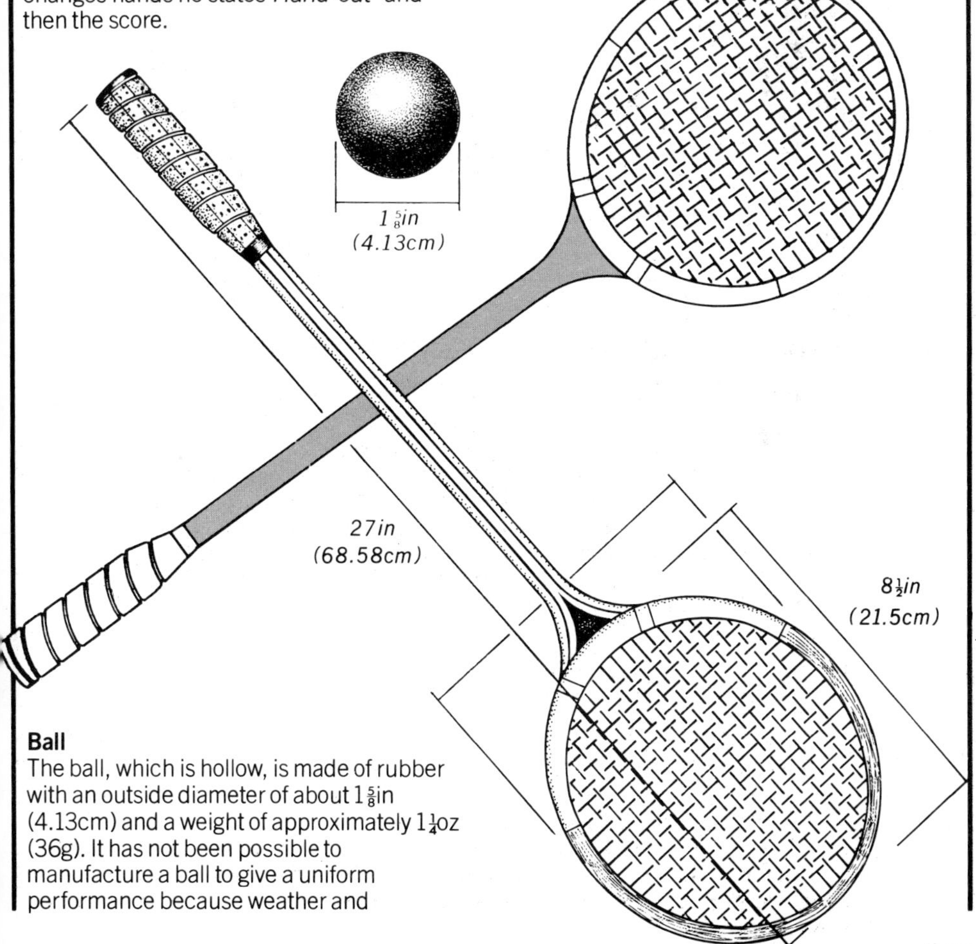

Ball
The ball, which is hollow, is made of rubber with an outside diameter of about 1⅝in (4.13cm) and a weight of approximately 1¼oz (36g). It has not been possible to manufacture a ball to give a uniform performance because weather and atmospheric conditions affect the balls greatly. Most British manufacturers produce 4 varieties of ball, ranging from the very slow for very hot conditions, to the fast for cold conditions. Most top tournaments use the very slow ball.

Racket
The squash racket has a smaller head than the badminton racket. The length must not exceed 27in (68.58cm). The head and handle are normally made of wood, and the head is strung with gut. Steel-shafted rackets have grown in popularity in recent years. The internal stringing area must not exceed 8½in x 7¼in (21.59 x 18.41cm).

Playing Area

Squash is usually played on a wooden surfaced court, enclosed on all 4 sides by 20ft (6.10m) walls. Into the end wall, is fitted a flush door through which players enter and leave the court.

The standard court is 32ft long x 21 ft wide (9.75m x 6.40m). Players have to hit the ball towards the front wall, which is divided into 3 sections by lines running its full width, and parallel to the floor. The 1st line is drawn 19in (48.26cm) from the floor. The area underneath is normally covered in tin to give a distinctive sound if the ball hits it. The area under the line is known as the tell tale. The 2nd line is 6ft (1.83m) above the floor, and this is known as the Cut Line. The 3rd line, 15ft (4.57m) above the floor indicates the upper limit at which the ball may be hit.

A line 7ft (2.13m) above the floor is marked on the back wall, and a diagonal line, down each side wall, joins the back-wall line and the

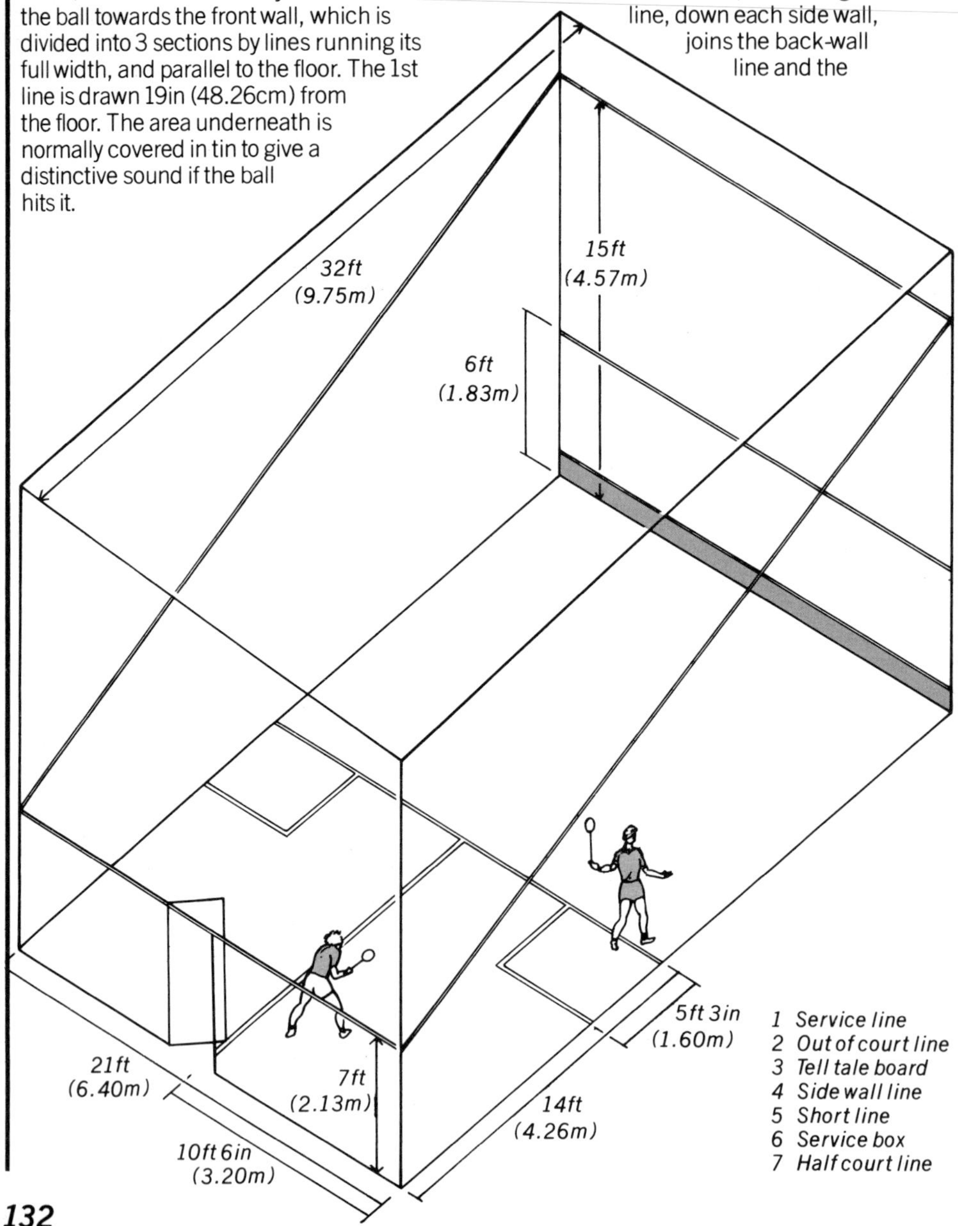

upper limit line on the front wall.

The floor is disected by a line 18ft (5.49m) from the front wall to divide the court into a front and back section. The back section is then divided in half by a short line that runs to the back wall. Service squares of 5ft 3in (1.60m) are marked in the front corner of each of the 2 back sections.

Service

A player can win a point only as the server. If he is the non-server and wins the rally he becomes the server.

The service is made from alternate service squares and onto the front wall in the area between the upper limit line and the tell tale line. The server must have at least one foot touching the floor inside the service square at the moment of serving. The ball must be thrown into the air and hit with the racket before touching the floor or wall, and must be hit directly at the front wall. After hitting the front wall it must return to the opposite rear court, but it can arrive there via a side wall. It must then bounce no more than once in the opposite rear court. The non-striker can, if he feels it to his advantage, volley the ball. As in tennis, the server is allowed one fault before making a good serve.

The server is referred to as *Hand-in* and the non-server as *Hand-out.*

If the server makes a fault, a bad service, the non-server *(Hand-out)* has the option to accept it as if it were good, and carry on play.

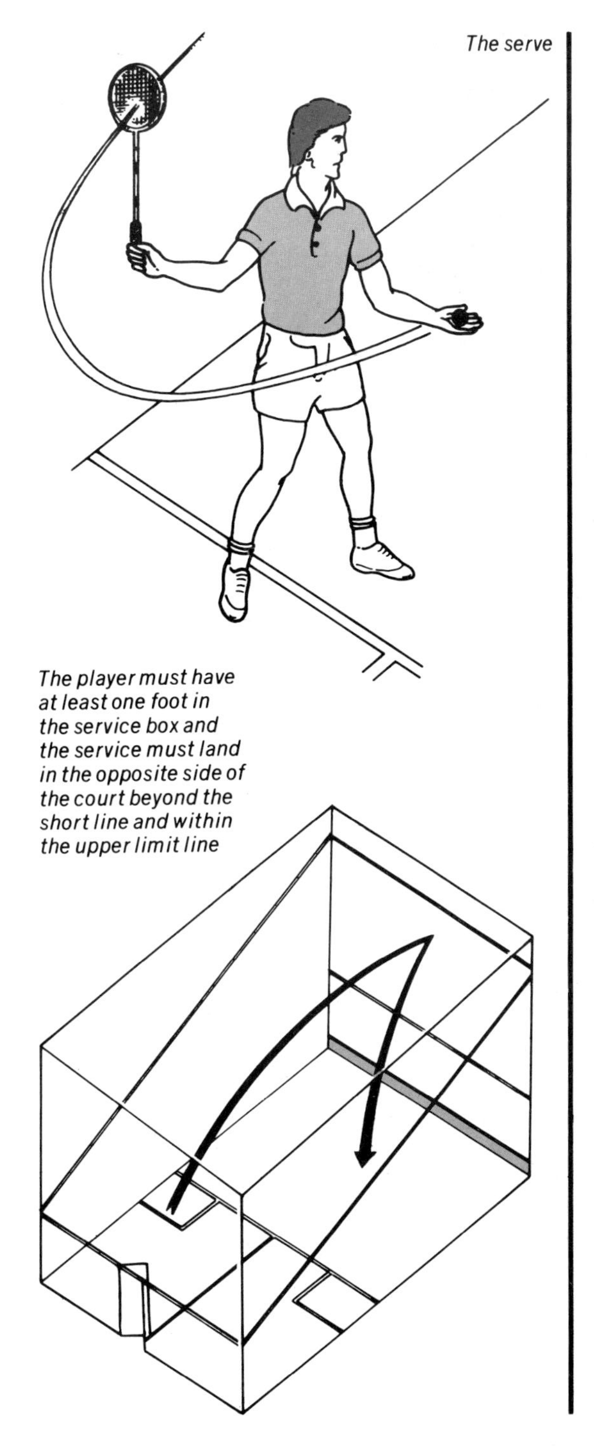

The serve

The player must have at least one foot in the service box and the service must land in the opposite side of the court beyond the short line and within the upper limit line

Let
If the striker hits the ball against his opponent before striking the front wall a let is called and the point replayed

Play

After the service the players hit the ball alternately. They can either volley the ball or allow it to bounce once only. Any ball hit above the upper limit line on the front wall, side-wall or back-wall line is 'out' and the point lost or invalid.

The basic tactic of squash is to get your opponent away from the centre of the court or the "T" by playing subtle drop shots to the front walls or powerful drives that cause the ball to end up near the back-wall.

It is one of the most stamina sapping of all sports and it is calculated that as many as 1000 stops, starts, twists and turns can occur in one hour's play.

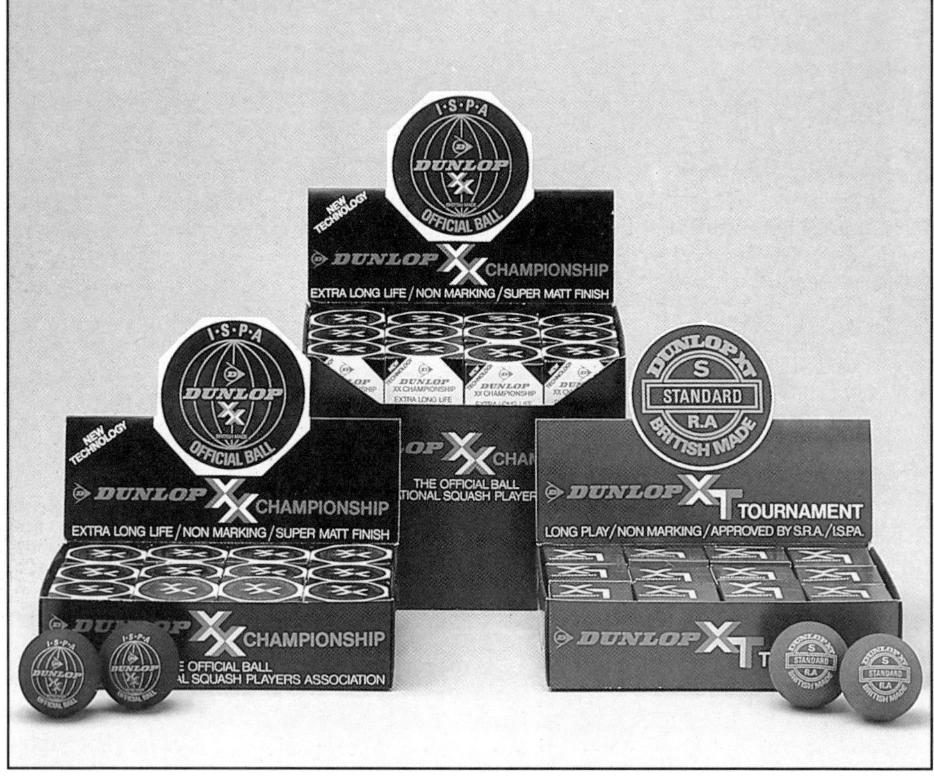

Clothing
Because the ball is black or green, players must wear white clothing, and to protect the playing surface, rubber-soled shoes.

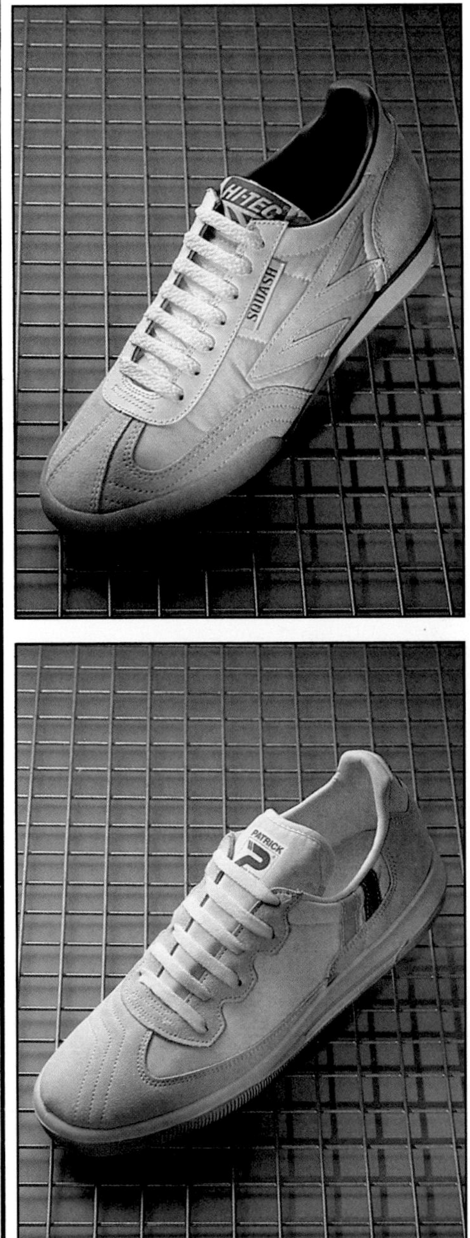

Racquetball

One of the fastest indoor games, Rackets, from which Squash was devised, is a game for two or four players. Rackets in its modern form developed in England in the middle of the 19th-century but a form of Rackets was played, outdoors, in the middle ages, although it was as much a variety of Handball as it was Rackets. The sport is very popular in Public Schools and the most famous court in England is at Queen's Club.

Object

To score more points than your opponent(s) by forcing him to make errors. Like many other racket and ball games, winning points can only be made from 'In-hand' i.e. when you are serving.

Duration

All games last until one player (team) has scored 15 points, and a singles match consists of five games while a doubles match lasts for seven games. If the scores reach 13-all the non-serving player may elect to set the game to three or five which means the winner is the first to reach 16 or 18, as the case may be. When the scores reach 14-all the non-server can elect to set the game to three if he so wishes.

Ball and Rackets

The ball which is hollow is made of rubber with an outside diameter of $2\frac{5}{8}$in (66mm). The rackets are similar to a squash racket but with a shortened handle and larger head.

Officials

The game is normally officiated by a marker who is positioned on the gallery overlooking the court. His role is to indicate when play is about to commence, to call when a shot is good or otherwise, to advise when faults occur, and to call the score in between points.

Playing Area

The floor of the playing area is normally asphalt or stone and measures approximately 30ft (9.1m) x 60ft (18.3m). The court is completely enclosed by four walls, 30ft (9.1m) high. On the front wall a service line is marked 9ft 8in (2.95m) from the floor. A wooden board 27in (68.58cm) high stretches the full length of the front wall. Right and left service boxes 7ft 6in (2.3m) square are marked 24ft (7.3m) from the back wall, and the back of the court is marked with two rectangular areas, each 15ft (4.6m) x 24ft (7.3m). These are known as the left and right courts.

Service

A spin of a racket decides who shall have first service, or be 'In-hand'. The server must have one foot in the service box and he must hit the ball on the front wall, above the service line. The ball must then rebound, either directly, or off another wall, into the opposing court, i.e. a service from the right service box, must land in the left court. The service alternates from right to left service box. In doubles play, partners alternate the service.

Play

After the service has been made a rally develops with the players alternatively hitting the ball above the wooden board. A rally comes to an end if (a), the ball does not hit the front wall above the wooden board (b) the ball bounces more than once on the floor (c) the ball is hit above the designated area for play, or (d) a player hits an opponent. A player may only win a point if he is 'In-hand'. If he wins the rally when not 'In-hand' he becomes the server. In a game of doubles, players must hit the ball alternatively, and in sequence.

Table Tennis

An indoor bat and ball game played by both men and women either as singles or in pairs.

Object
To score more points than your opponent by winning rallies.

Duration
Each match consists of a pre-arranged number of games, normally 5 in singles and 3 in doubles. The winner of each game is the first player to 21 points but, if the scores reach 20-20 then the game is not over until one player establishes a 2 point lead. If, however, the game is not ended in 15 minutes the *expedite system* can be introduced. This means that for the remainder of that game service is alternated point by point and the server is allowed a maximum of 13 strokes to win each point. If he does not, the point is automatically awarded to his opponent. Once the expedite system has been introduced, all subsequent games in the match are played to this format.

Players

Men and women play singles and doubles, partnering members of their own sex (men's doubles or women's doubles) or members of the opposite sex (mixed doubles).

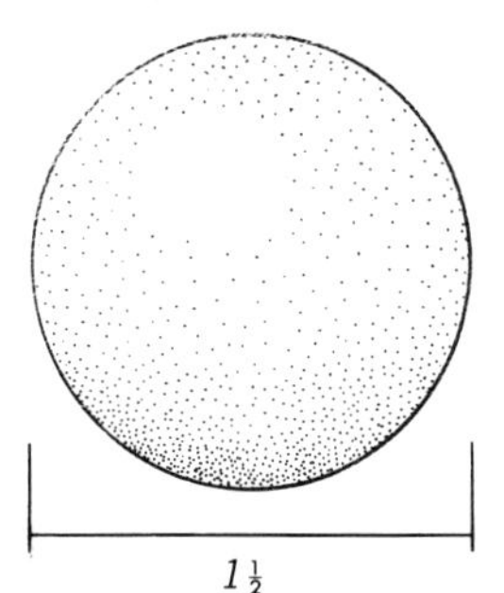

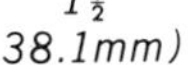

Ball

Table tennis has the smallest ball of all bat and ball games with a diameter of just 1½in (38mm) and a weight of less than half an ounce (2.5gm). It is made of celluloid or similar plastic material and is white or yellow, and matt.

Bat

Development of the bat has brought new techniques into the sport. It may be of any size but the blade must be made of wood and of even thickness, flat and rigid. Any covering must be ordinary pimpled rubber – with the pimples on the outside having a maximum thickness of 2mm ($\frac{3}{32}$in) or sandwich rubber, a layer of sponge rubber backed by pimpled rubber facing inwards. The maximum thickness of this bat is 4mm per side. Alternatively a combination of the two coverings, one on either side, can be used. This type of bat offers the player greater variety of play. Since the introduction of the sandwich bat, the game has used more speed and spin.

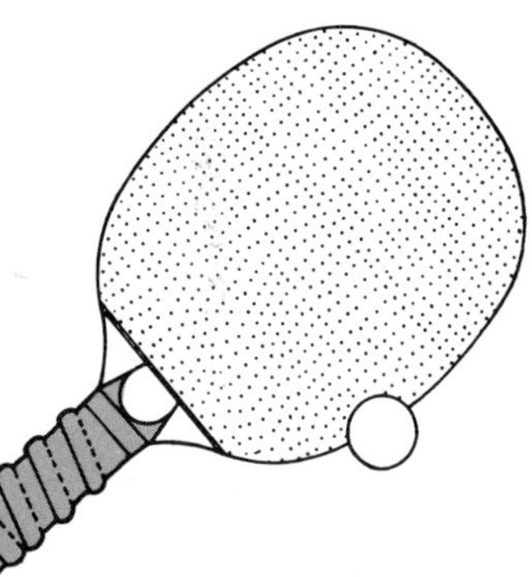

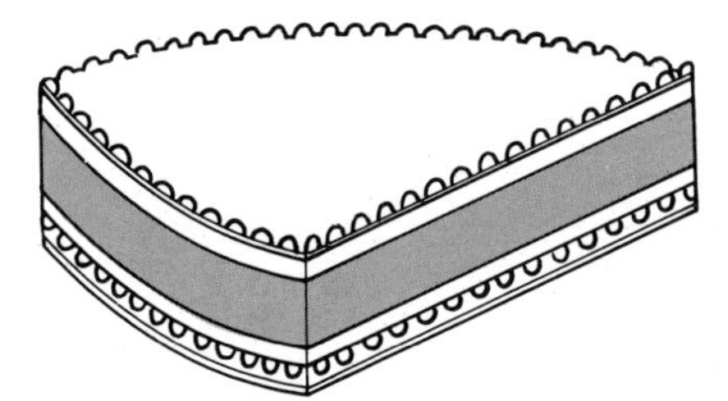

The surface of the bat can be plain pimpled rubber of a total thickness not exceeding $\frac{3}{16}$in (2mm)

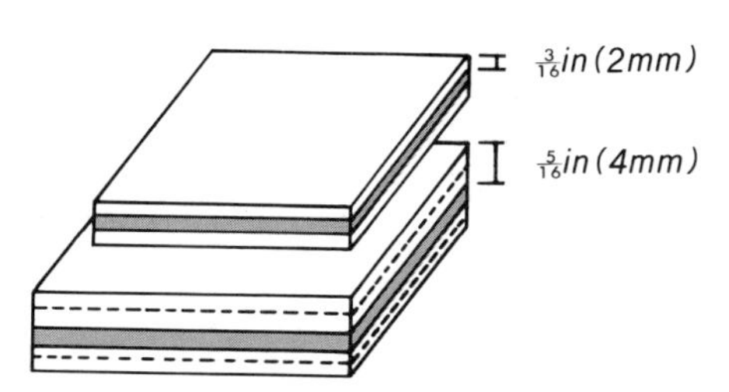

The back of the bat is exempted from the covering rules

Officials
The game is controlled by an umpire who is assisted by a scorer. The umpire is responsible for judging who won each rally and resolving matters of dispute. When calling out the score he should always call the server's score first.

Playing Area
A table 9ft (2.74m) long by 5ft (1.525m) wide. The surface is wooden and painted green with white line markings around the perimeter. The top of the table is 2ft 6in (76cm) above the level of the floor and the middle of the playing area is disected by a 6in (15.25cm) high net that overhangs the table by 6in (15.25cm) at each side. The minimum playing area required in international matches is 46ft (14.02m) x 23ft (7.01m). For doubles play, a white line from the end of the table to the net divides each half of the table.

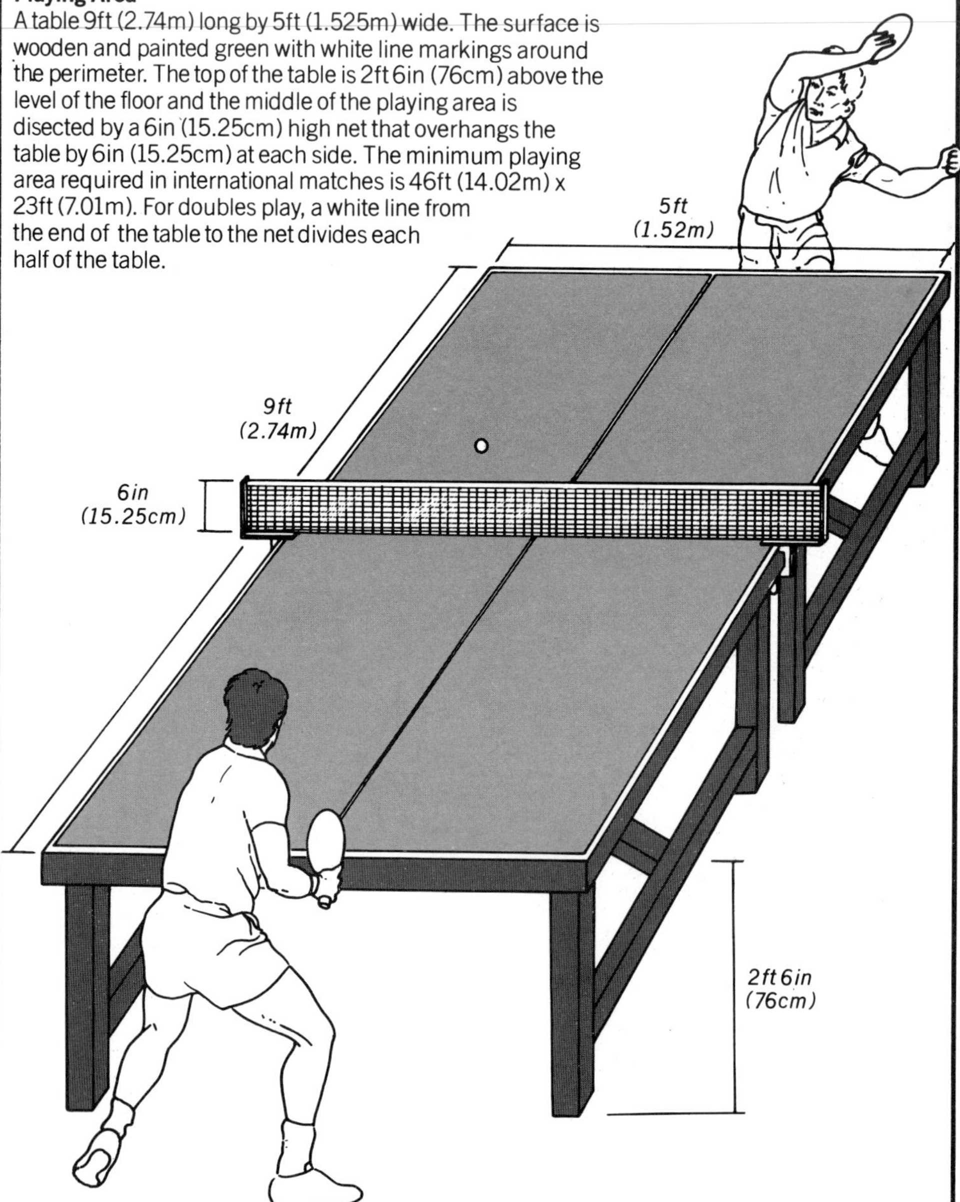

Service

Each player serves for 5 points, and then passes service to his opponent. They alternate throughout each match, unless the scores reach 20-all, when service swaps after each point. If the expedite system has been introduced the service again alternates after each point.

For a fair service the ball must be held in the palm of the server's hand and no attempt be made to spin it with the fingers. The ball must be thrown up into the air and struck with the bat. It must bounce once on each side of the net. Failure to make a clean service results in one point being awarded to the opposite player(s). Unlike lawn tennis, only one service attempt is allowed unless the ball strikes the net and lands in the opponent's half of the table, in which case a *let* is called and the serve taken again.

In doubles play the serve always takes place from right-hand half-court to right-hand half-court. It must land in the server's half of the court before landing in the receiver's half of the court. Once the serve is complete, the ball can be returned to any part of the table.

The service

The service sequence in doubles is: the player to serve first of one pair (1a) serves to the player who serves first of the second pair (2a); 2a then serves to 1b; 1b serves to the fourth player, 2b; and 2b serves to 1a.

Each player is allowed 5 serves, as in singles, with each team taking turns. The server will serve to the same opponent throughout his 5 serves. The receiving player then becomes the server and he serves to the previous server's partner, and so on. The same order of play is maintained throughout each game and players must hit the ball in that sequence – no player from one side is allowed 2 consecutive hits of the ball during any one rally.

Play

Once the serve has been completed successfully the ball is hit over the net alternately by the players. The ball must not be volleyed at any time; or the point is lost. The ball must always bounce once only before being returned over the net. The rally comes to an end if a player strikes the ball into the net, or his shot fails to hit the table on his opponent's side of the net or it hits the table twice on a player's own side of the net. Ends are changed after each game. If a match goes to the final game (3rd or 5th), ends are changed when a player reaches a score of 10.

Grips

There are two main styles of grip, the *Western grip* adopted by the European nations and the *Eastern penholder* developed by Asian players. The penholder's main advantage is that only one side of the bat is used. Time is saved through not having to turn the bat around to play forehand or backhand shots. In the *Western grip* players have to adjust when changing from backhand to forehand. The choice comes down to personal preference and comfort as both grips are as effective as each other.

1, 2 & 3
A player fails to make a good service

4, 5 & 6
A player fails to make a good return

Clothing
Players must wear coloured clothing (shirts and shorts, or skirts for ladies). White attire is not permissable as it would clash with the ball.

Vest and shorts should be of lightweight, absorbent materials. Footwear is similar to squash, with crepe or rubber soles for good grip.

A table tennis racket can be of any size, shape or weight, but the blade must be flat and rigid and made of wood. Pimple rubber and sandwich rubber – a layer of cellular rubber covered with an outer layer of pimpled rubber – impacts spin on the ball.

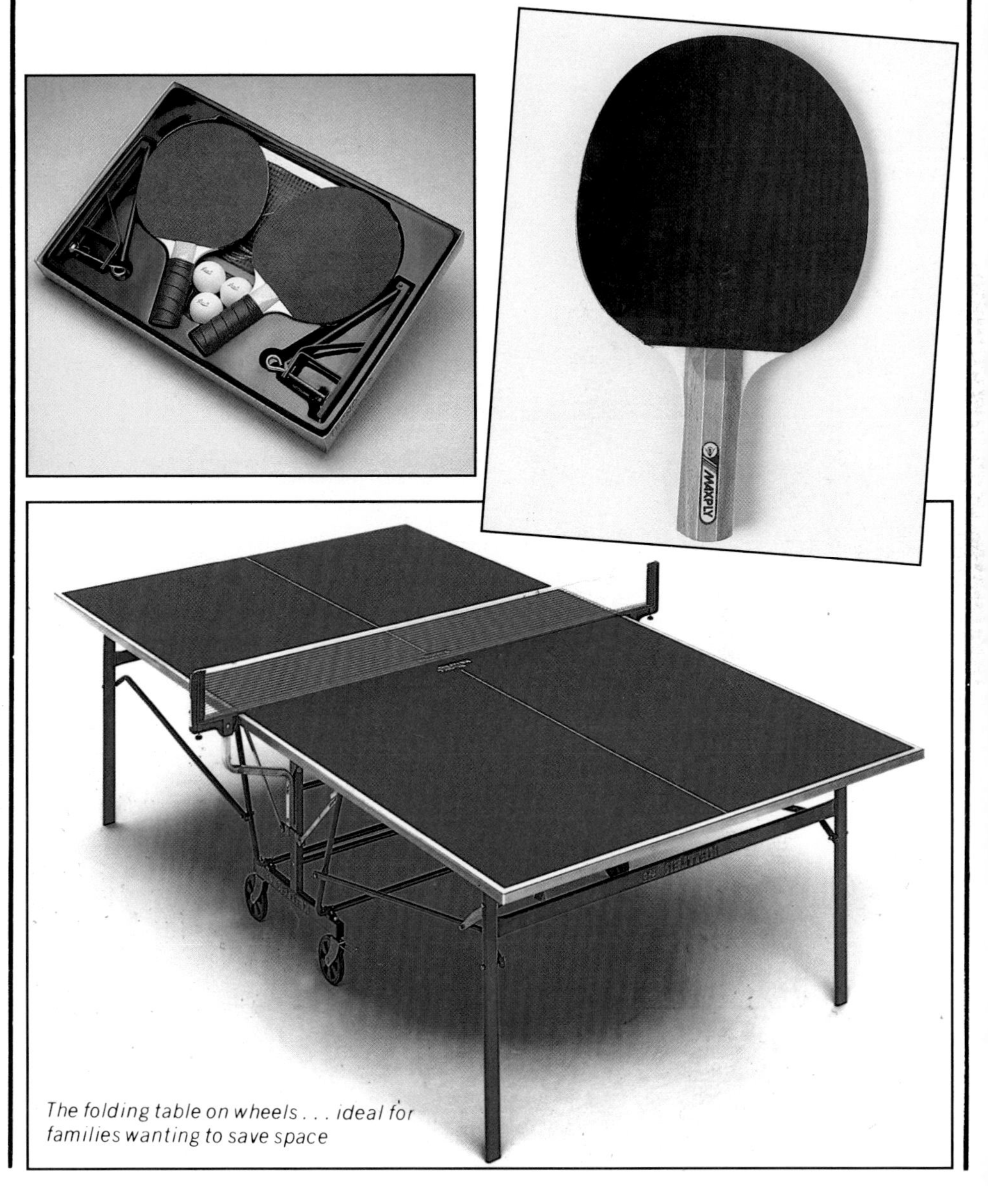

The folding table on wheels . . . ideal for families wanting to save space

Tennis

The most popular of all bat and ball games, tennis is played indoors or outdoors by 2 players as singles, or 4 players as doubles. Tennis dates back to the 14th century when a ball game was invented in France, which did not use a raquet, but a hand. Strung rackets were first seen in the 15th century. Lawn tennis, more or less as it is known today, was popularized in the mid-18th century and, in 1877, the first Wimbledon Championships were held.

Object
To win rallies and gain points by successfully hitting the ball over the net and into your opponent's half of the court.

Duration
There is no time limit on each match – which consists of a predetermined number of sets, either 3 or 5. The first player to take 2 or 3 sets accordingly, is the winner. To gain a set a player must win 6 games, with a margin of at least 2 games over his opponent. Play continues until one player wins by 2 clear games. But, in all sets, except the final set, a tie-break is introduced when the scores reach 6-all. See *Tie Break* page 148.

Players
Men and women play tennis, both individually against members of their own sex (singles), as pairs against members of their own sex (men's/women's doubles) and as mixed pairs against another mixed pair (mixed doubles).

Ball
The tennis ball is made of rubber and surrounded by wool, or a man-made substitute with stitchless seams. The pressure inside varies to suit differing conditions, but this pressure quickly alters during a match. Before the start of a major tournament all balls are kept refrigerated to 20 degrees centigrade and the balls in play (normally 6 at a time) are changed after the first 7 games, and every 9 games thereafter. The diameter of the ball must be between 2½-2⅝in (6.35-6.67cm) and its weight between 2-2⅛oz (56.7-60.24g). When dropped from a height of 100in (2.54m) on to a concrete base, it must bounce 53-58in (1.35-1.47m). Most tennis balls are white, but yellow ones are also widely used these days, particularly in floodlit matches.

Officials
An umpire has the overall control over a match and has the power to overrule this linesmen who judge whether a ball is in or out. He is also responsible for keeping score and of ensuring good behaviour is maintained on the court.

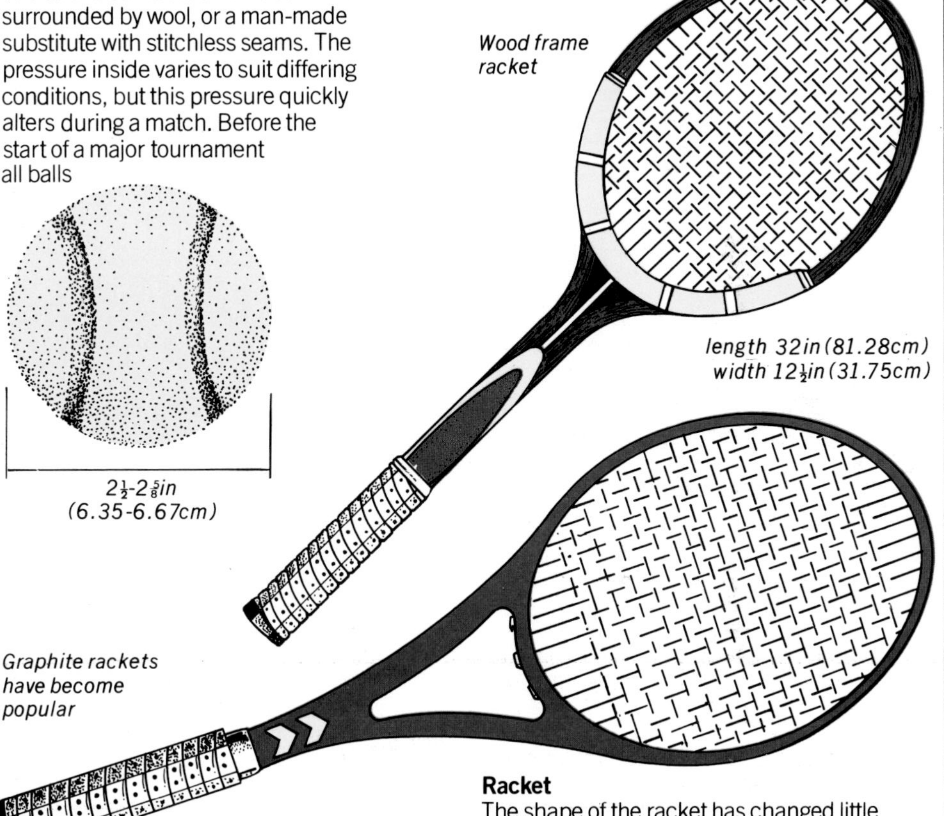

Racket
The shape of the racket has changed little over the years, but the materials in its manufacture have altered.

The frame may be of any material, shape or weight. Most are either wood or metal, and the average weight is around 13-14oz (368.55-396.9g). The length of the racket must not exceed 32in (81.28cm) in length and 12½in (31.75cm) in width. It is normally 26-28in (66.04-71.12cm), and the head approximately 12in x 10in (30.48cm x 25.4cm). The head is strung with natural gut or an artificial substitute.

Playing Area

There are 5 main playing surfaces for tennis – grass, wood, concrete, clay, and artificial grass. Each has its own characteristics and style of play varies accordingly.

The court measures 78ft in length x 36ft wide (23.77m x 10.97m). Inside are two 4ft 6in x 78ft (1.37m x 23.77m) strips known as the tramlines. This part of the court is for doubles only, and any ball landing in that area during singles is deemed to be out of the court. A centre net divides the court into 2 halves. The net, stretching the full width of the court, is 3ft (0.92m) high at the centre and 3ft 6in (1.07m) high at the posts. Each half of the court is divided by a centre line 21ft (6.40m) from, and parallel to, the net and a further line disects the area from the net to the centre of the service line. These markings create 2 service courts – a left and right service court. Each is 13ft 6in (4.11m) wide.

At either end of the court is a base line, with a marker indicating its centre.

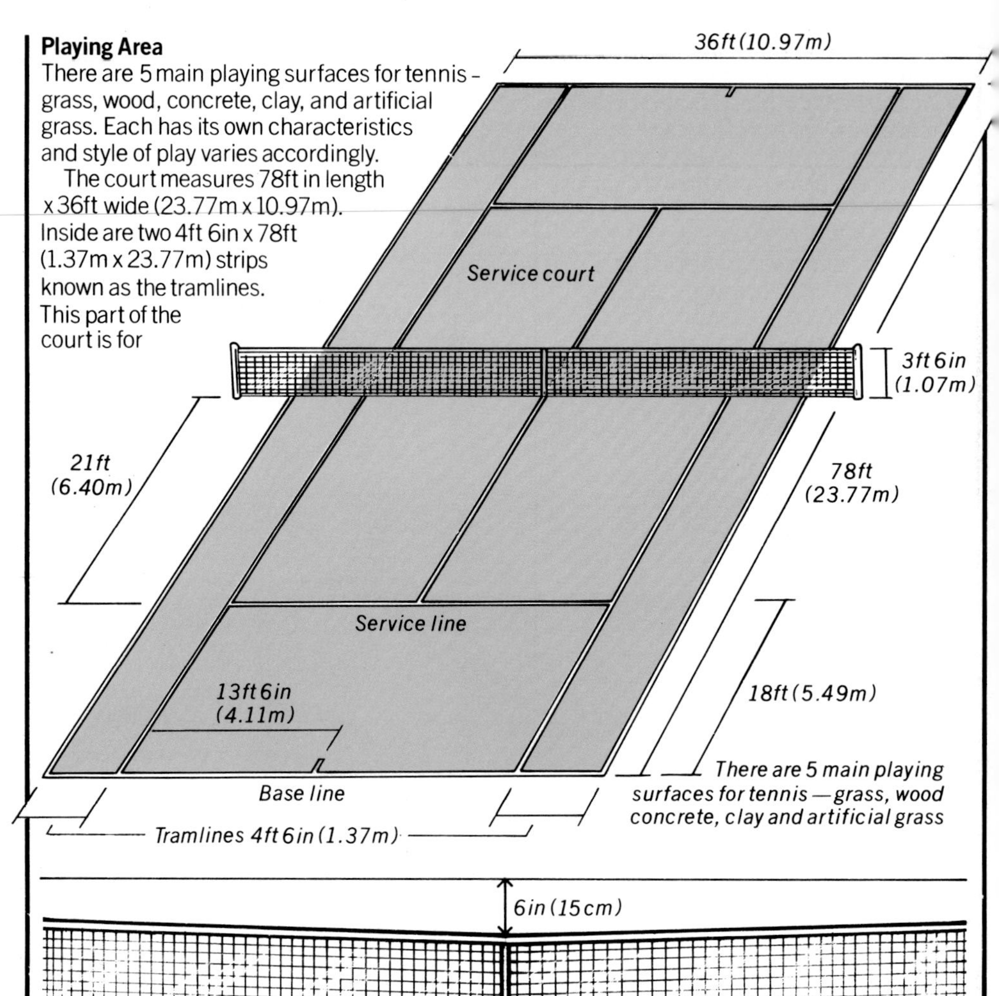

There are 5 main playing surfaces for tennis — grass, wood concrete, clay and artificial grass

Starting Play

A toss of a racket, usually decides which player serves first. He is allowed 2 attempts at a good service and, if he fails, he is said to have *double faulted.* To serve properly the ball must be thrown into the air and hit, usually overarm, with the head of the racket. To start, the server stands behind the base line at the end of his right hand court and to the right of the mark indicating the centre of the base line. For the serve to be good the ball must clear the net and bounce once in his opponent's right service court. The receiver can then attempt to return the ball to any part of the court, (except the tramlines if a singles game). The rally continues until the ball is not successfully returned over the net by one player, allowed to bounce twice on one side of the net, or the ball first lands outside the confines of the playing area. After the point is won, the same player serves again, but from the left court, to the opposing left service court.

The serve

All changes of serve start from the right hand court

He alternates like this until the end of the game. All changes of service start from the right court.

At the end of the first game the players change ends and thereafter at the end of every 2 games.

A player does not have to let the ball bounce in his half of the court, he may volley the ball if he so wishes, but he must not volley the service return.

Scoring

Unlike some other racket and ball games, points are won by a player whether he serves or not. The scoring in tennis is also unique in that points are not added in the order of 1-2-3-4 etc, but by 15,30,40. It is believed this system derived from the quarters of a clock with the 45 being corrupted to 40. A player must win 4 rallies to take a game. If he does so without his opponent winning a rally then the scoring sequence will be: 15-love, 30-love, 40-love, Game. The love is believed to be of French origin from the word *l'oeuf* (egg) which represents the figure 0. If the scores in any one game reach 40-all the score is said to be *deuce* then one player must win 2 consecutive rallies in order to win the game. After 40-40 the winner of the point is said to have 'advantage'. If that same player wins the next rally he wins the game. If he loses, the score reverts to deuce.

Tie-Break
The tie-break was authorised in 1970 to avoid lengthy sets. The tie-break comes into operation when scores reach 6-6. The player scheduled to serve does so, but for the first point of the tie-break only. Thereafter the players take 2 services each alternately. The scoring in the tie-break reverts to the standard 1-2-3 etc and the first to reach 7 points wins the tie-break and the set 7-6. But a tie-break must be won by 2 clear points or scoring continues beyond 7 until one player does so.

Net-cord judge

Doubles Play
The tram lines are used in doubles play. The opening server serves first from the right court as in singles. At the end of each rally the server moves to the left-hand court (while his team-mate usually stands somewhere near the net in the right court). The opposing team do not change sides at the end of each point, moving instead in their own half from net to baseline as non-receiver and receiver. At the end of the game, the player who received the first service serves first to the non-serving member of the opposing team, and so on. Once the serve has been completed the players can hit the ball in any order, providing each team hits it alternately.

Let
If a service hits the top of the net and bounces into the appropriate court then the serve shall be taken again without any loss to the server. If, however, the ball lands outside the appropriate court, it is deemed to be a bad service. If the ball hits the net during a normal rally *'let'* is not called by the net-cord judge and play continues unless the ball is deflected out of court.

Foot Fault
Both feet must be behind the base line at the serve, and must remain behind the line until contact has been made by the racket with the ball. Otherwise a foot fault is called and the service lost. A ball landing on the line marking the perimeter of the court is *in.*

Foot fault

Clothing
Some of the attractive modern tennis wear using subtle colour along with the traditional white

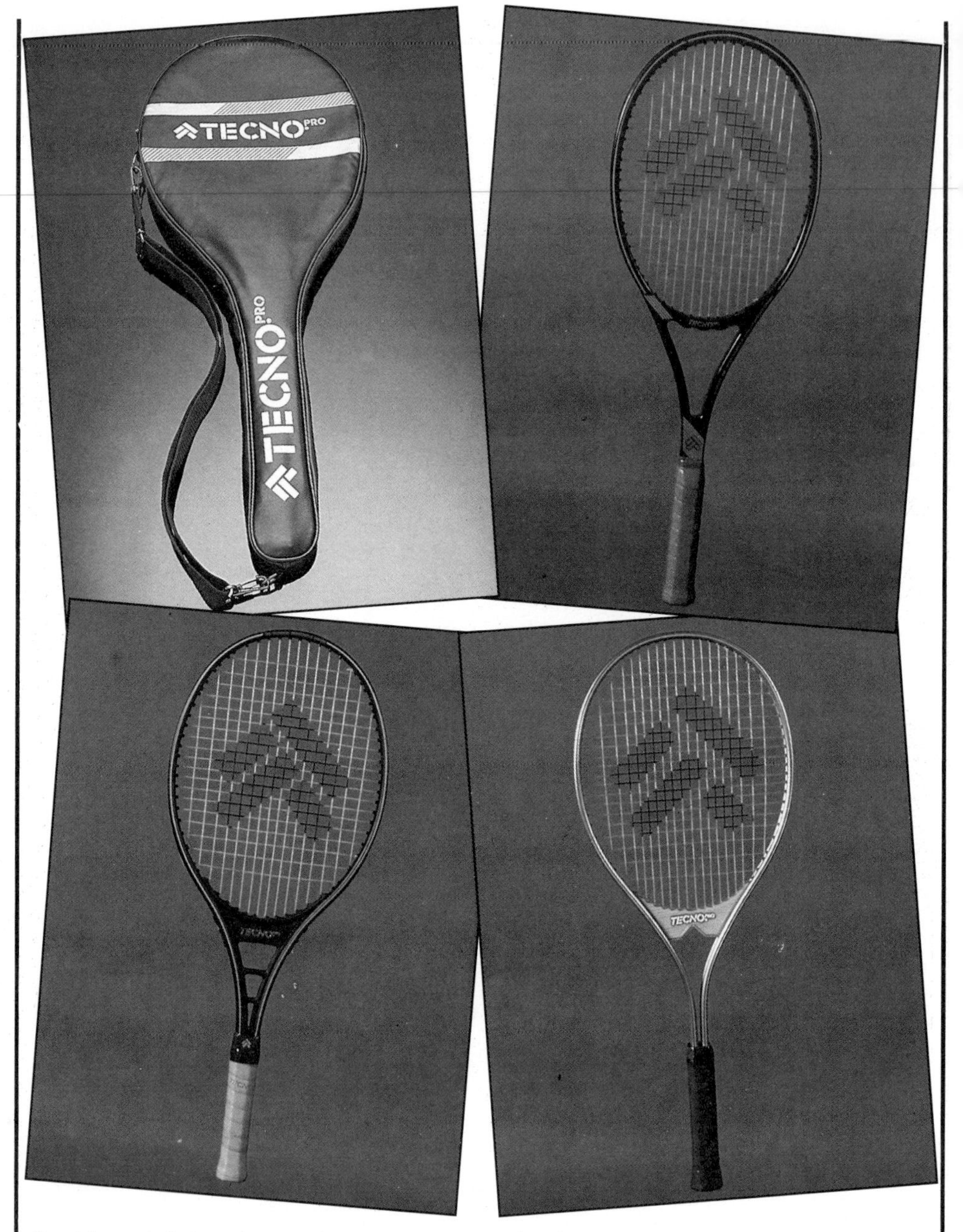

Graphite rackets have become increasingly popular but some players still prefer the feel of the traditional wood. Beech is used for less expensive rackets. Ash is also very pliable for heads. Hickory is used for shafts, and walnut and mahogany for the veneers and inlays.

The best strings are made from sheep gut although the Australians used beef gut also. It takes six to eight sheep to string one racket.

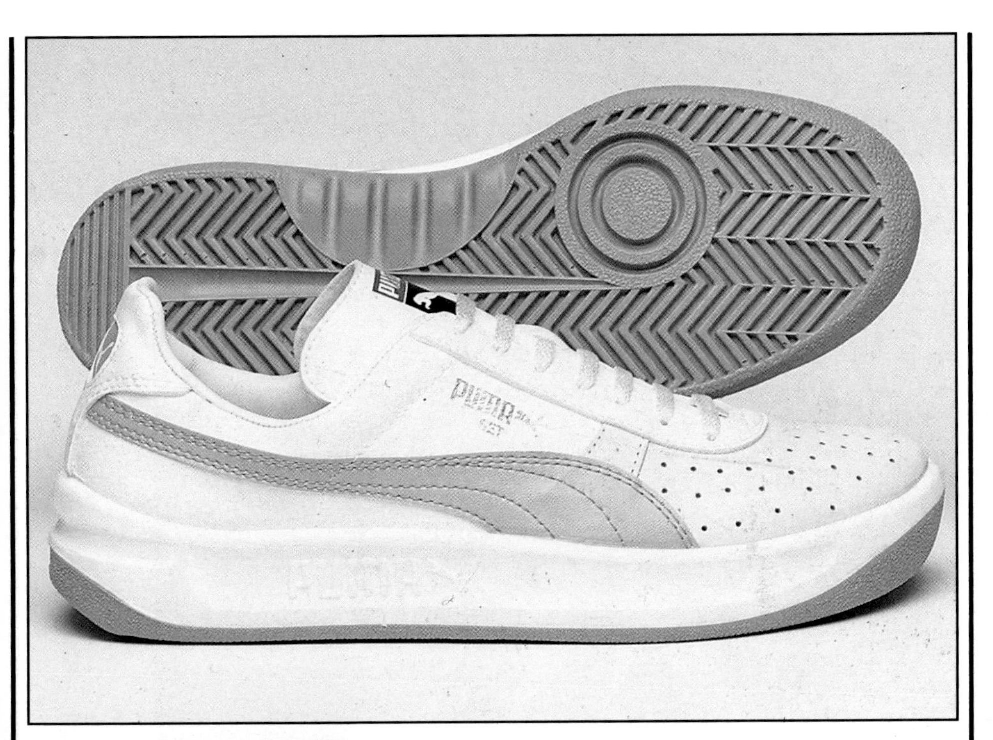

Tennis footwear is lightweight, ventilated, rubber-soled and high-backed to protect the heel.

Volleyball

A game for 2 teams each with 6 players, which can be played indoors or outdoors, although most major tournaments are held indoors. Volleyball was devised by W.G. Morgan, a physical training instructor at the Holyoke, Massachussetts, YMCA in 1895, who invented the game for older members who found basketball too energetic.

Object
To put the ball over the net and get it to land in your opponent's half of the court, or force your opponent to play the ball out of the court or into the net, and thus give you points.

Duration
There is no time limit. A game is normally played over the best-of-3 or 5 sets. A set comes to an end when one team reaches 15 points or, if the scores are level at 14-all, when one team takes a 2-point advantage.

Teams

6 players plus 6 substitutes.

All 6 substitutes are allowed to take part in the game during each set either individually, or collectively. A substituted player may re-enter the court, but only in the position he was in at the time of being replaced.

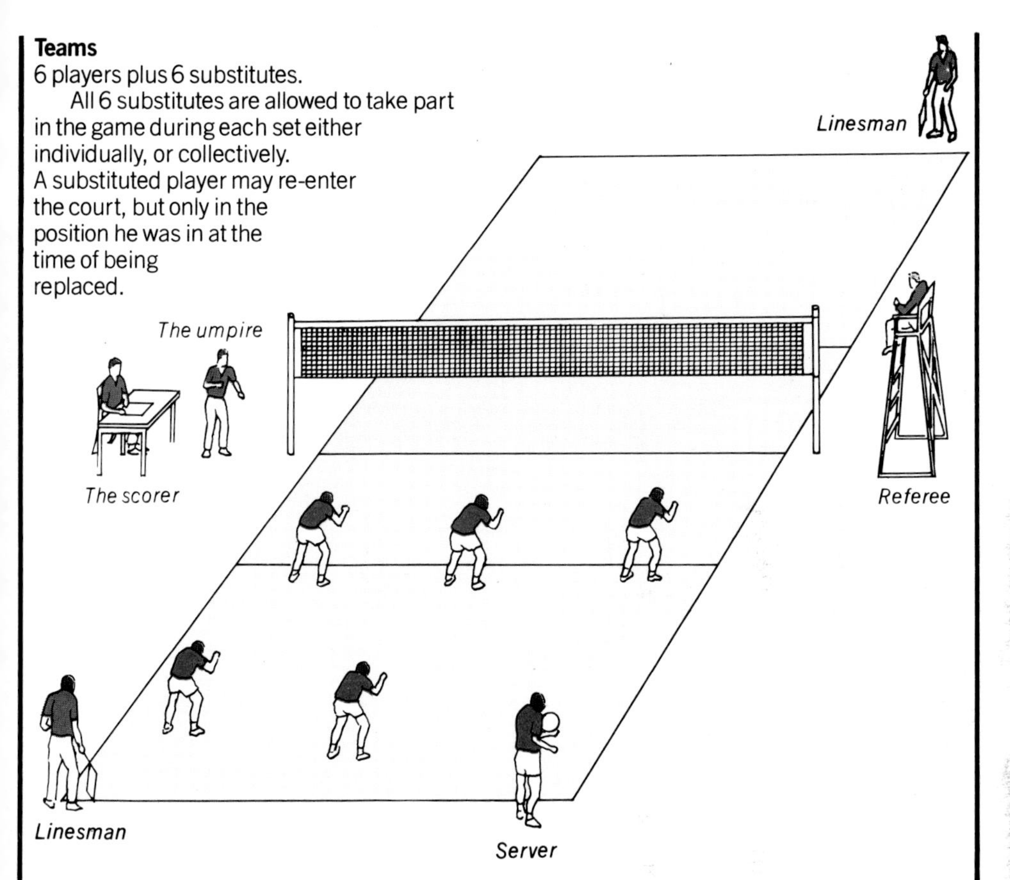

Each player wears a number between 1-6 and, at the start of the game takes up the position as shown in the diagram. When a team wins the serve, all members rotate one place to the right in a clockwise direction. The other team do not move, and the team winning the serve do not move again until such time as they regain the serve after losing it.

Officials

A referee controls the match. He takes up a position close to, and above, one end of the net. He is assisted by an umpire and scorer, who are both situated on the opposite side of the court and to the referee, and 4 judges seated by the side lines and base lines.

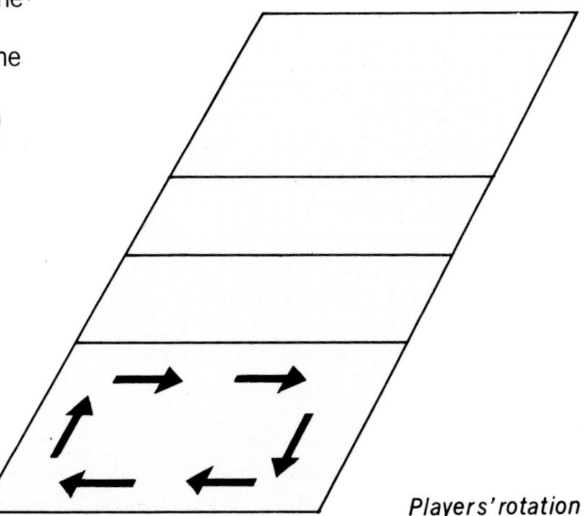
Players' rotation

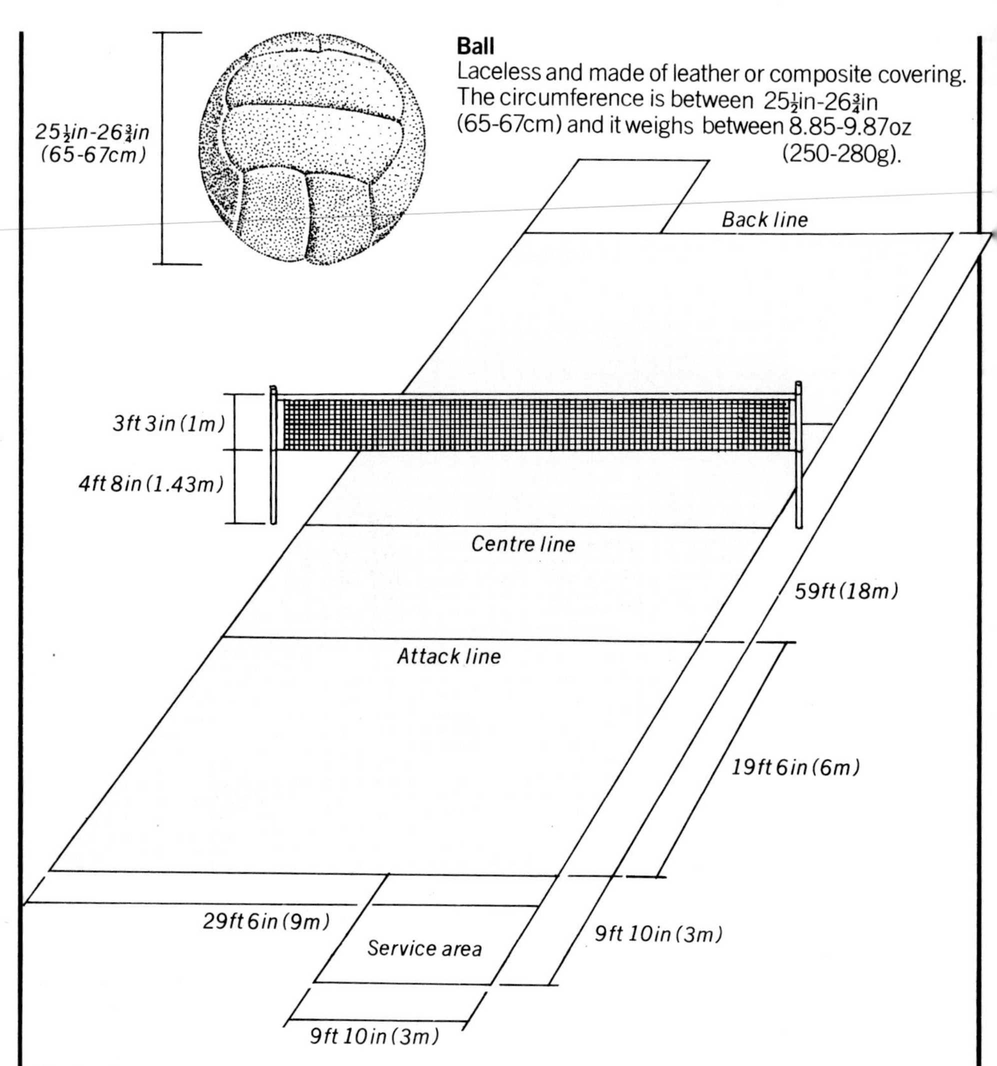

Ball
Laceless and made of leather or composite covering. The circumference is between 25½in-26¾in (65-67cm) and it weighs between 8.85-9.87oz (250-280g).

Playing Area
Volleyball is played on a rectangular area 59ft x 29ft 6in (18m x 9m) and divided into 2 equal square courts by the fine centre line. An attack line is marked across the court 9ft 10in (3m) from, and parallel to, the centre line. Above the centre line there is a 3ft 3in (1m)-deep stretched net which spans the width of the court. The height of the net at the centre is 7ft 11⅝in (2.43m) for men and 7ft 4⅛in (2.24m) for women. Ideally there should be a clear space of 9ft 10in (3m) around the perimeter of the court and an air space of 23ft (7m) above it. Each court has a service area attached to the right hand corner measuring 9ft 9in (3m) square.

Service
The first server stands in the service area and hits the ball with his hand or arm over the net. All other players must line up in the specified format. Once the service is completed the players can move around the court at random. Only the serving team can win a point. Should the non-serving team win the rally they take service.

Underarm serve *Tennis serve* *Hook serve*

Play

The receiving side are allowed to touch the ball 3 times before returning it over the net. It can be returned on the first touch but most teams attempt to manoeuvre the ball to one of their front line players to 'smash' into the opposing half. Once the ball has been grounded, not been returned over the net, or been returned but landed outside the court, the rally is over and a point won, or service changed depending upon who served at the time. Teams change ends after each set and when one team reaches 8 points in the final set.

When two opponents simultaneously commit a foul the point is replayed

Each team may play the ball three times before sending it over the net

No individual may hit the ball in successive strokes in any one rally and the ball must always be struck cleanly with the arms or hand with no indication of holding or carrying.

The smash is the most likely stroke to win a point. This is when team members have lifted the ball for a front line player to climb high and smash it down into the opposing court. The counter is the *'block'* whereby one or all of the opposition front line players jump simultaneously to block the smash and force it back over the net.

Players are penalized for the following infringements:

Net fault . . . touching the net with any part of their body while the ball is in play.
Screening . . . obstructing an opponent's view of the server.
Foot Fault . . . when the server stands on, or in front of, the service line when the ball is struck. Or when any player's foot is entirely in the opposing half of the court.

Time Outs
The captain or coach of one team may call a time-out at any stage in order to revise team tactics. Two time-outs per team, each lasting 30 seconds, are allowed in each set.

Blocking
One or more players may block an opponent's shot. Any blocking player is entitled to a second play at the ball

Clothing
Clothing should consist of a vest or jersey, shorts, and rubber or leather pliable shoes, without heels. Players can, at the referee's discretion, play without footwear. Dangerous articles must not be worn. Players of each side must be dressed in the same colour and the numbers worn on their chest and back must be 15.24cm (6in) high and 5.08cm (2in) wide. Many players prefer long-sleeved shirts to give protection to the elbows and arms. Players may wear protective pads on their knees.

INTERSPORT®

Intersport – over 200 shops in these towns:

England

Andover – Cole & Son
Bath – Intersport;
Terry Warner Sports
Barkingside – Link Sports
Barnsley – Don Valley Sports
Berwick-on-Tweed – Intersport
Beverley – Arco Sports & Leisure
Bexleyheath – Woodruff Sports
Birmingham – Harry Parkes;
Sportsco *(2 branches)*
Boston – J. Morley Sports
Bracknell – Topsports
Bradford – Carters of Bradford
Bristol – Edwards Sports House
Burgess Hill – Herbert Sports
Bury – Sam Taylor
Bury-St-Edmunds – McNeil Sports
Cambridge – McNeil Sports
Cheadle Hulme – F. R. Monkhouse
Chelmsford – Pope & Smith
(2 branches)
Cheltenham – Terry Warner Sports
Chester – Jack Sharp
Chesterfield – Ian Buxton Sports;
Intersport
Chichester – Hargreaves Sports
Chippenham – Cole & Son
Christchurch – Priory Sports
Clacton on Sea – McNeil Sports
Colchester – Harpers Sports
Corby – Sportsworld *(2 branches)*
Coventry – Aubrey Hill
Davies – The Sports People
Crawley – Herbert Sports
Croydon – Sports Chalet
Darlington – T. Reed & Sons
Derby – Redmayne & Todd
Devizes – Cole & Son
Doncaster – Don Valley Sports;
Fit Kit Sports
Dorking – Seymours
Dudley – Sportsco
Dunstable – Intersport
East Dereham – Rudd Sports
East Grinstead – Herbert Sports
Enfield – Bernards World of Sport
(Pearsons Sports Dept)
Epsom – Seymours
Exeter – De Paula Sports;
Wessex Sports
Fareham – Hargreaves Sports
Felixstowe – McNeil Sports
Gateshead – Dixon Sports;
Monument Sports
Gloucester – Terry Warner Sports
(2 branches)
Grantham – Intersport
Gravesend – Smallcombe Sports
Grays – Smallcombe Sports
Great Yarmouth – Doughty's
Grimsby – Freetime
Guildford – Intersport
Harlow – Intersport
Harrow – Mancini Sports
Hartlepool – Dixon Sports
Hastings – Wisdens
Hemel Hempstead – Peter Spivey
Hertford – Intersport
Hitchin – Sportorama
Hoddesdon – Intersport/Sportstime
Huddersfield – Bakers Sports Centre
Hull – Arco Sports & Leisure
Huntingdon – Sports & Fashions
Ilford – Link Sports
Ipswich – McNeil Sports
Keighley – Willis Walker
Kettering – Sportsworld
Kings Lynn – Rudd Sports
Kirby-in-Ashfield – Tebbutt Brown
Leeds – Herbert Sutcliffe; Sportstime
Leicester – Sportsco; Tebbutt Brown
Letchworth – Sportorama
Lincoln – Jack Sharp;
Sullivan Sports *(2 branches)*
Loftus – Pykes Sports
London – Ashley Intersport NW11
Gordon Grose Sports
(2 branches) EC4, N13
Intersport (West 8 Sports) W8
Link Sports – E15
Intersport (Lucas Sports) –
Brent Cross
Intersport – W5
Multisports *(5 branches)* EC1,
EC2, EC3, WC1, WC2
Sports Chalet – SE13
Sun & Snow – SW3
Williams Sports & Leisure N12
Loughborough – Harry Prince;
Sportscene
Loughton – Link Sports
Luton – Bernard's World of Sport
Macclesfield – Trevor Bayley Sports

Maidenhead – Ashley Intersport
Manchester – Tyldesley & Cooke
Mansfield – Intersport , Packer Sports
Mexborough – Don Valley Sports
Middlesbrough – Monument Sports
Newark – Intersport
Newcastle-upon-Tune – Dixon Sports *(2 branches)*
Intersport St. James
Monument Sports
Northampton – Sportsworld
Norwich – R. G. Pilch
Nottingham – Redmayne & Todd *(2 branches)*
Sportsco
Old Rossington – Don Valley Sports
Orpington – Woodruff Sports
Oxford – Elmer Cotton Sports;
Elmer Cotton
Penrith – Sportscraft
Peterborough – Intersport;
Hereward Sports
Poole – Ted MacDougall Sports
Portsmouth – Hargreaves Sports
Rayleigh – Pope & Smith
Redcar – T. Reed & Sons
Ripley – G. B. Sports
Rochdale – Trevor Butterworth Sports
Runcorn – Jack Sharp
Scunthorpe – Jim Ball Sports
Intersport
Sidcup – Woodruff Sports
Solihull – Ray Hitchcocks
Southsea – Hargreaves Sports;
Peter Anderson Sports
St. Albans – Riders
St. Helens – Sullivan Sports
Stafford – Sportsco
Stevenage – Sportorama
Sutton Coldfield – Sportsco
Swindon – Terry Warner Sports
Taunton – Wessex Sports
Walsall – Sportsco
Waltham Cross – Intersport/Sportstime
Wakefield – Craven Sports
Warrington – Bullough Sports
Washington – Monument Sports
Watford – Peter Spivey
Wellingborough – Sportsworld
West Bromwich – Sportsco
West Wickham – Young Folk Sports
Whitby – Pykes Sports
Wilmslow – Gilberts Sports
Winchester – Hargreaves Sports
Wolverhampton – Sportsco *(2 branches)*
Worcester – Centurion Sports
Yeovil – De Paula Sports
York – T. Mitchell

Scotland

Avlemore – Cairdsport
Ayr – Finnies *(2 branches)*
Buckhaven – Intersport
Carnoustie – David Low Sports
Cowdenbeath – Intersport
Dundee – David Low Sports;
Intersport
Dunfermline – Intersport
Edinburgh – Thornton Sports;
Intersport *(2 branches)*
Galashiels – Sportswise; Intersport
Glasgow – Greaves Sports;
Lumleys Sports;
Scotsport (Glasgow)
Glenrothes – Intersport
Hamilton – Viking Sports; Intersport
Inverness – Intersport
Kelso – Sportswise
Kirkcaldy – Intersport
Rutheglen – Intersport
St. Andrews – Intersport
Stirling – Intersport

Wales

Barry – Astoria Sports
Bridgend – Gilesports
Cardiff – Edwards Sports House;
Gilesports *(3 branches)*
Cwmbran – Gilesports
Merthyr – Astoria Sports
Neath – Sports Outfitters
Newport – Edwards Sports House;
Gilesports
Penarth – Astoria Sports
Pontypridd – Edwards Sports House
Porth – Astoria Sports
Swansea – Central Sports;
Edwards Sports House;
Gilesports

Northern Ireland

Ballymena – S. S. Moore
Belfast – S. S. Moore
Dungannon – Intersport Craigavon
Portadown – Intersport Craigavon

Isle of Man

Douglas – Turners *(2 branches)*
Douglas – The Sports Centre

For full address details see Intersport entry in Yellow Pages under sports goods shops or by shop name in your local telephone directory.

Acknowledgements

First Editions and Ian Morrison would like to thank the following:

The Diagram Group for illustrations
Allsport Photographic for photography
Giorgio Moltoni for artwork
David Emery for the Introduction